HERE AND THERE
AMONG THE PAPYRI

FRAGMENTS FROM A PAPYRUS ROLL OF LATE THIRD CENTURY,
CONTAINING ST. JOHN XV. 25–XVI. 2 AND XVI. 21-31.

Discovered at Oxyrhynchus (Oxyrh. Pap. x. 1228), and gifted by the Egypt Exploration
Society to Glasgow University Library

HERE & THERE AMONG THE PAPYRI

BY

GEORGE MILLIGAN

D.D. (ABERDEEN), D.C.L. (DURHAM)

PROFESSOR OF DIVINITY AND BIBLICAL CRITICISM IN THE
UNIVERSITY OF GLASGOW

WITH A FRONTISPIECE

Wipf and Stock Publishers
EUGENE, OREGON

Wipf and Stock Publishers
199 West 8th Avenue, Suite 3
Eugene, Oregon 97401

Here and There Among the Papyri
By Milligan, George
ISBN: 1-59244-182-3
Publication date: March, 2003
Previously published by Hodder and Stoughton Limited, January, 1923 .

J. H. M.

τῷ ἀγαπητῷ καὶ συνεργῷ μου
εὐχαριστήριον

Here and There among the Papyri

Foreword

THIS small book is addressed in the first instance to that wide and ever-increasing public who are keenly interested in the study of the New Testament, and are anxious to know more of the bearing of the papyrus discoveries, of which they hear so much, on its language and literature. Every effort has, therefore, been made to avoid unnecessary technicalities, and no Greek words or phrases have been used without their English equivalents. At the same time, even though it involves some repetition of matter I have published elsewhere, I have tried to give at least an indication of the principal points in the whole field of inquiry. For the sake of those who wish to pursue the subject further, full references are given in the Notes to the sources from which the documents made use of are drawn, and also to some of the most accessible literature dealing with the questions at issue.

It only remains to tender my grateful thanks to Professor A. S. Hunt for the readiness with which he has placed his unsurpassed knowledge of the papyri at my disposal, to my colleague Professor R. S. Rait for his kindness in reading the proofs and making many valuable suggestions, and to the Rev. A. W. Stevenson, Balshagray, for various press corrections.

Here and There among the Papyri

Selected Bibliography

This Bibliography is in no sense intended to be exhaustive, but aims only at suggesting a few books which may be of use to those who wish to make a beginning in the study of the Papyri in their relation to the New Testament.

TEXTS.—As regards Texts, a start may be made with the small selection of eleven *Greek Papyri*, edited with notes by H. Lietzmann (Cambridge, Deighton Bell & Co., 1905. 6d.). The second edition of S. Witkowski's *Epistulae Privatae Graecae* (Leipzig, Teubner, 1911) contains 72 letters of the Ptolemaic period with a Latin commentary, and a useful conspectus of grammatical peculiarities. In R. Helbing's *Auswahl aus Griechischen Papyri* (in the *Sammlung Göschen*, 1912) 24 texts are annotated in German. And in *Selections from the Greek Papyri*, 2nd Edit. (Cambridge University Press, 1910. 7s. 6d.) 55 miscellaneous texts are edited by the present writer with translations, notes, and a general introduction.

These collections may be followed by *Grundzüge und Chrestomathie der Papyruskunde*, a large selection of important documents, edited, with valuable historical and legal introductions, by L. Mitteis and U. Wilcken (Leipzig, Teubner, 1912. Formerly 40s.). But, in addition, students are strongly advised to acquire gradually some of the principal original collections of papyrus texts. Amongst these they will find specially helpful the Graeco-Roman Memoirs including the *Oxyrhynchus Papyri*, issued by the Egypt Exploration Society (13 Tavistock Square, London, W.C. 1) under the notable editorship of Professor B. P. Grenfell and Professor A. S. Hunt. By a subscription of two guineas a year, they will not only further the general work of exploration, but themselves become possessors of the annual volume of texts, while a further payment of 28s. will entitle them to *The Journal of Egyptian Archaeology* (issued to the public at 50s.).

LEXICONS.—No Lexicon of the Papyri has yet appeared, but their significance in relation to the vocabulary of the New Testament has been skilfully utilized by Professor Souter in his *Pocket Lexicon to the Greek New Testament* (Oxford, Clarendon Press, 1917. 3s. 6d.), and they are constantly referred to in Professor G. Abbott-Smith's recently published *Manual Greek Lexicon of the New Testament* (Edinburgh, T. and T. Clark, 1922. 21s.), which has been received with so much deserved favour. Reference may also be permitted to *The Vocabulary of the Greek Testament* by J. H. Moulton and G. Milligan (London, Hodder & Stoughton, 1914-), of which four parts have already appeared (i. A, 6s.; ii. B to Δ, 7s. 6d.; iii. E-Θ, 7s. 6d.; iv. I-Λ, 10s.), a systematic attempt to illustrate the New Testament vocabulary from the papyri and other non-literary sources.

GRAMMAR.—On the side of Grammar, Dr. J. H. Moulton's *Grammar of New Testament Greek*, Vol. I. *Prolegomena*, 3rd Edit. (Edinburgh, T. and T. Clark, 1919. 10s.) is indispensable, and should be studied along with the two parts of Vol. II., prepared for the press with such care by Professor W. F. Howard—Part i. General Introduction,

Sounds and Writing, 7s.; Part ii. Accidence. 10s.; Part iii., completing Vol. II., is in active preparation. Mention must also be made of Professor A. T. Robertson's monumental *Grammar of the Greek New Testament in the Light of Historical Research*, 3rd Edit. (London, Hodder & Stoughton, 1919. £2 2s.), which is practically a *Thesaurus* of all that relates to the Greek of the New Testament. Though dealing primarily with the Septuagint, Mr. St. John Thackeray's *Grammar of the Old Testament in Greek*, Vol. i. Introduction, Orthography and Accidence (Cambridge University Press, 1909. 12s. 6d.), is of great value for New Testament students.

INTRODUCTION.—In the field of Introduction, many interesting points, vividly presented, will be found in Dr. J. H. Moulton's popular lectures on the New Testament, published under the title *From Egyptian Rubbish-Heaps* (London, Kelly, 1916. 3s. 6d.), and the bearing of the papyri on the origin and early history of our New Testament writings is discussed by G. Milligan in the Croall Lectures for 1911-12, *The New Testament Documents* (London, Macmillan, 1913. 12s. 6d.). Unfortunately Professor Deissmann's fascinating volume *Light from the Ancient East* (London, Hodder & Stoughton, 1910), to which so many references are made in the following pages, is now out of print; the writer informs me that he is engaged on a new German edition (published as *Licht vom Osten*). A smaller book by Dr. Deissmann, *New Light on the New Testament from Records of the Graeco-Roman Period* (Edinburgh, T. & T. Clark, 1907. 4s.), is still procurable, as are also his pioneer *Bible Studies*, 2nd Edit. (Edinburgh, T. & T. Clark, 1901. 10s.), and his Cambridge lectures on *The Philology of the Greek Bible* (London, Hodder & Stoughton, 1908. 5s.) with their numerous bibliographical notes. Those who read German may be referred to the comprehensive *Einführung in die Papyruskunde* by W. Schubart (Berlin, Weidmann, 1918), and to the same writer's popular sketch, *Ein Jahrtausend am Nil* (Berlin, Weidmann, 1912).

Other literature dealing with the Papyri, in addition to what is mentioned in the Notes at the close of the present volume, will be found in the introductory material to *Selections from the Greek Papyri*, and the full titles of the principal Papyrus Collections, with the contractions by which they are ordinarily referred to, are prefixed to the different Parts of *The Vocabulary of the Greek Testament*.

Here and There among the Papyri

Contents

	PAGE
FOREWORD	vii
SELECTED BIBLIOGRAPHY	ix

CHAPTER I

THE GREEK PAPYRI: THEIR CHARACTER, DISCOVERY AND PUBLICATION

INTEREST OF THE PAPYRI	1
PAPYRUS AS WRITING MATERIAL	2
PAPYRUS DISCOVERIES	7
PUBLICATION OF PAPYRI	15
CLASSIFICATION OF PAPYRI	19
Literary	19
Biblical and Theological	22
Non-literary	23

CHAPTER II

THE PAPYRI AND THE ORIGINAL NEW TESTAMENT WRITINGS

NEW TESTAMENT AUTOGRAPHS	27
Outward Appearance	28
Addresses	29

xiv *Here and There among the Papyri*

	PAGE
LETTERS OR EPISTLES	32
DICTATION	38
Shorthand	45
METHOD OF READING	47
QUESTIONS OF STRUCTURE	50
PAPYRUS CODEX	53

CHAPTER III

"COMMON" GREEK AND THE NEW TESTAMENT

"NEW TESTAMENT" GREEK	55
VARIOUS EXPLANATIONS	56
ITS REAL CHARACTER	57
ANTICIPATIONS OF THIS VIEW	59
NEW GAINS	62
Vocabulary	63
Examples	64
Grammar	79
LITERARY CHARACTER OF NEW TESTAMENT	79

CHAPTER IV

THE SURROUNDINGS OF THE NEW TESTAMENT WRITERS

THE ORDINARY MEN AND WOMEN OF THE TIME	82
THE GRAECO-ROMAN WORLD	84
THE CENSUS PAPERS	85

	PAGE
FAMILY LIFE	89
Husbands and Wives	89
Parents and Children	92
Education	96
Slaves	97
SOCIAL LIFE	101
TAXATION	103
PETITIONS	105
SENSE OF BEREAVEMENT	106
SENSE OF SIN	108
QUESTIONS IN TEMPLES	109
MAGICAL PAPYRI	110

CHAPTER V

CHRISTIAN DOCUMENTS ON PAPYRUS

CHRISTIANITY IN EGYPT	113
NEW TESTAMENT TEXTS	115
NON-CANONICAL TEXTS	123
Sayings of Jesus	128
THEOLOGICAL WORKS	132
LITURGICAL WORKS	133
Hymns	135
Prayers	136
Creeds	138
CHURCH ORGANIZATION	139
Libelli	142

	PAGE
CHRISTIAN LETTERS	144
QUESTIONS IN CHURCHES	149
AMULETS	150
NOTES	153

INDEXES

1. AUTHORS AND SUBJECTS	173
2. NEW TESTAMENT REFERENCES	177
3. GREEK WORDS	179

NOTE.—The small figures, as *e.g.* [1] at the end of the second paragraph on p. 2, refer to the Notes at the end of the volume.

The Greek Papyri: their Character, Discovery and Publication

Interest of the Papyri.—Few archaeological discoveries in recent years have awakened more widespread interest than the countless papyrus documents which have been recovered from the sands of Egypt. And if the extravagant claims sometimes advanced on their behalf may at once be set aside, there can be no doubt that they have thrown light of a very welcome character on the form and language of our New Testament documents, and on the historical surroundings in which these books took their rise. Before, however, turning to these and similar points, it is necessary to form as clear an idea as possible of the appearance and character of the papyri themselves, and to recall briefly the history of their discovery and publication for the sake of those who have been unable to follow that history in detail.

Papyrus as Writing Material.—In itself, the word papyrus is the name of a reed-plant (*Cyperus papyrus L*), which at one time grew in great profusion in the river Nile, and gave its name to the writing material or " paper " of antiquity, formed from it. The stem of the papyrus plant was cut into long thin strips, which were laid down on a flat table and soaked with Nile water. A second layer was then placed crosswise on the top of the first, and the two layers were pressed together to form a single web or sheet. After being dried in the sun, and scraped with a shell or bone to remove any roughness, a material not unlike our own brown paper was produced.[1]

The size of the papyrus sheets varied considerably, but for non-literary documents a common size was from nine to eleven inches in height, and from five to five and a half inches in breadth. When more space than that afforded by a single sheet was required, a number of sheets were joined together to form a roll. A roll of twenty sheets seems to have been a common size for selling purposes, but this could easily be extended if desired. One roll has actually been found, running to the length of one hundred and forty-four feet. On the other hand, smaller quantities than twenty sheets would be readily procurable.

The side of the papyrus on which the fibres ran horizontally, or the *recto*, as it came to be technically known, was from its greater smoothness generally preferred for writing, while the back, or the *verso*, was reserved for the address, at any rate in the case of letters. But when space failed, the *verso* could also be utilized, as shown in a long magical papyrus in the British Museum, in which nineteen columns are written on the *recto*, and the remaining thirteen on the *verso*.

It is tempting to find in this practice an explanation of the reference in Rev. v. 1. to the book of woes as " written within and on the back." So numerous, that is, were these woes that one side of the papyrus roll could not contain them, and they had to be carried over to the other. But, while this is a fair interpretation of the words, it is right to notice that the word rendered " on the back " (ὄπισθεν) may refer not to what precedes, but to what follows. If so, the document was not a roll at all, but in the form of a codex or book, each leaf being placed on the top of the other, and, because it was sealed " on the back " or " on the outside," its contents could not be known, until the seals were loosed.

In any case we have abundant evidence of the use of the *verso*, when fresh papyrus was not available, as when a man writes a letter on the back of a business document, explaining that he had been unable at the moment to find a " clean sheet " (χάρτιον καθαρόν),[2] or as when the back of the official notification of the death of a certain Panechotes is used for a school-exercise or composition, embodying such maxims as " do nothing mean or ignoble or inglorious or cowardly," written in a beginner's hand and much corrected.[3]

In other cases, before the *verso* has been so used, the original contents of the *recto* have been effaced or washed out, a practice which again adds point to a familiar verse.

In Col. ii. 14, we read that our Lord " blotted out the bond written in ordinances that was against us, which was contrary to us," and the verb used for " blotted out " (ἐξαλείψας) is the technical term for " washing out " the writing from a papyrus sheet. So complete was the forgiveness which Christ by His work secured, that it completely cancelled the old bond, that had hitherto been valid against us, for it bore our signature (χειρόγραφον). He made the bond as though it had never been (cf. Exod. xxxii. 32 f., Rev. iii. 5).

As regards other writing materials, a reed-pen (γραφικὸς κάλαμος ; cf. 3 Macc. iv. 20) was prepared, much as we now prepare a quill, while the ink (μέλας : cf. 2 John 12) was made from a mixture of charcoal, gum and water. The marvellous way in which the ink has preserved its colour invariably attracts attention, and shows that anything in the nature of adulteration must have been unknown. A first century letter, chiefly about writing materials, refers to the " ink-pot " (τὸ βρόχιον τοῦ μελανος).[4]

The character of the handwriting naturally

varied with the nature of the document and the education of the scribe. But the task of decipherment can rarely be said to be easy, partly owing to the frequent use of contractions and partly to the numerous *lacunae* or gaps caused by the brittle nature of the material. The restoration of the letters or words that have thus dropped out demands the exercise of the utmost patience and skill. And those who have had an opportunity of inspecting some of the originals can only marvel that intelligible transcriptions have been made from them at all.

When then we speak of papyri, we are to think simply of rolls or sheets of paper of this character, which had been put to all the many and various purposes to which paper as a writing material is put amongst ourselves, while the addition of " Greek " distinguishes the papyri written in that language from the Aramaic or Latin or Coptic papyri which have been similarly recovered. We need only add that the earliest dated Greek papyrus we possess belongs to year 311-310 B.C. (cf. p. 89), and that from that time an almost continuous chain of documents carries us far down into Byzantine times. Their special interest, however, for the student of the New Testament from a linguistic point of view may be said to stop with the close of the third, or the beginning of the fourth, century of the Christian era.

Papyrus Discoveries.—When we turn to the discovery of these documents, the fact that, with the exception of some calcined rolls from Herculaneum, which were brought to light as far back as 1752 and the following years,[5] papyri have been found only in Egypt is due simply to the marvellously dry climate of that country. A certain number, more particularly those of a literary character, have been recovered from their original owners' tombs. The *Persae* of Timotheos, for example, the oldest Greek literary manuscript in existence, dating, as it does, from the fourth century B.C., was found near Memphis in the coffin of a Greek soldier, by whose side it had been deposited in a leathern bag. And an Homeric roll, now in the Bodleian Library, Oxford, used to be exhibited along with a lock of the hair of the lady with whom it had been buried. Other rolls have been found in earthen jars in the ruins of temples or houses, thus strangely recalling the prophecy of Jeremiah : " Thus saith the Lord of hosts, the God of Israel : Take these deeds, this deed of the purchase, both that which is sealed, and this deed which is open, and put them in an earthen vessel ; that they may continue many days" (xxxii. 14, R.V.). And yet others have come from a still more romantic source.

It was a common practice in Egypt to cover the upper part of a mummy with a head-piece and breastpiece, roughly moulded to the human form. In the construction of this, layers of old papyri were frequently used as backing or stuffing, the whole being coated over with painted plaster. And now by the careful removal of this plaster, and treatment with the " pure " paraffin which is sold for medical purposes, the underlying papyri have been brought to light, and yielded up their contents to the skill and perseverance of the explorers.

But the great mass of papyri come from the rubbish heaps, rising sometimes to a height of twenty to thirty feet, on the outskirts of old Egyptian towns and villages. Possibly out of a feeling of reverence for the written word, the inhabitants did not as a rule burn their old papers, but threw them out on these heaps. There they were quickly covered over with the fine desert sand, and, so long as they were above the damp level of the Nile, have remained practically uninjured down to the present day. For the most part they consist of single sheets, or fragments of sheets, sometimes no larger than a postage stamp, but occasionally whole baskets of official documents are found, which had been cleared out *en masse* from public archives or record offices. And everyone will recognize the absorbing interest attaching to these scraps of paper, discarded as useless by their first writers and owners, and on which no eye has looked for many hundreds of years, but which now, as original documents, recreate and revivify the past for us in a way which nothing else could do.

The earliest finds in Egypt of which we have any knowledge took place in 1778, when some Arabs, digging for their own purposes in the Fayûm district, accidentally came upon about fifty rolls in an earthen pot; but, unable to find purchasers, they destroyed them on account, it is said, of the aromatic smell they gave forth in burning. Only one roll was saved which, from passing into the hands of Cardinal Stefano Borgia, came to be known as the *Charta Borgiana*. The contents are of little general interest, being merely an account of the forced labours of the peasants on the Nile embankment at Arsinoë in the year 191-192 A.D., but the papyrus will always have the significance of being the first Greek papyrus to be published in Europe.[6]

In the year 1820 further finds, dating from the second century B.C., were made in the neighbourhood of Memphis and Thebes, some of which throw vivid sidelights on the internal administration of the great Temple of Serapis at the former place. The next year saw the first important literary find, which was fittingly an Homeric manuscript containing

Iliad xxiv. ; and this was followed in 1847 by the recovery of a large roll, containing three of the lost orations of Hyperides, a contemporary of Demosthenes, who had been hitherto only a name in the Lexicons.

These discoveries were largely accidental, and even in 1877, when great masses of papyri were unearthed on the site of Arsinoë, the ancient Crocodilopolis, most of which went to Vienna to the collections of the Archduke Rainer, the work still suffered from want of method and supervision, with the result that a large proportion, probably quite a half, of the papyri found by natives in this district perished altogether.

It was not until 1889-90 that a beginning was made in systematic exploration when at Gurob Professor Flinders Petrie extracted a large number of papyri from Ptolemaic mummy-cases, and brought them home to England. Owing to the conditions under which they were found, the work of decipherment was often exceedingly difficult, and Dr. (afterwards Sir John P.) Mahaffy, by whom they were skilfully edited, has given a graphic account of the process, and the thrills with which it was accompanied. " Gradually pieces of a Platonic dialogue emerged, which presently we determined to be the *Phaedo*; then a leaf of a tragic poem, identified beyond question as the *Antiope* of Euripides; and with these were many legal or official documents with dates, which arrested and surprised us. For instead of the later Ptolemies, or the Roman emperors, whose names occur in the Greek papyri already found, here we could read nothing but *Ptolemy the son of Ptolemy Soter*, and *Ptolemy the son of Ptolemy and Arsinoe, brother gods*—in other words, the second and third kings in the series (280-220 B.C.). There could then be no doubt whatever of the significance of the discovery. As there were no dates to be found later than the third Ptolemy, it followed with moral certainty that the classical texts mixed up with these documents could not be younger than 220 B.C." [7]—to be reckoned therefore amongst our earliest classical manuscripts.

To the same period of exploration belong

such important literary finds as the lost work of Aristotle on *The Constitution of Athens*, copied out on the back of a farm-bailiff's accounts, which are dated in the eleventh year of Vespasian, that is 78-9 A.D.; the *Mimiambi* or *Mimes* of Herondas, which reproduce with photographic exactness the ordinary, and often sordid, details of the everyday life of the third century B.C.; and about thirteen hundred lines of the *Odes* of Bacchylides, a contemporary of Pindar, and a nephew of the Simonides for the recovery of whose works Wordsworth longed in a well-known sonnet:

> O ye, who patiently explore
> The wreck of Herculanean lore,
> What rapture! Could ye seize
> Some Theban fragment, or unroll
> One precious, tender-hearted, scroll
> Of pure Simonides.[8]

But significant though these discoveries were, their interest in public esteem was largely eclipsed by the results of the digging carried on by Dr. Grenfell and Dr. Hunt at Oxyrhynchus, the ancient Behneseh, in the winter of 1896-97 and the following years.

The attention of the two English explorers had been attracted to the spot in the expectation that early fragments of Christian literature might be found there, in view of the important place which Oxyrhynchus occupied in Egyptian Christianity in the fourth and fifth centuries. And their prescience was rewarded, for, amongst the papyri recovered on the second day, was a crumpled leaf, written on both sides in uncial characters, amongst which Dr. Hunt detected the somewhat rare Greek word for " mote " (κάρφος). This suggested to him the " mote " of our Lord's Saying in the Sermon on the Mount (Matt. vii. 3-5) ; and, on further examination, he found that he had in his hand a leaf out of a very early collection of Sayings attributed to Jesus, some of which corresponded closely with the canonical Sayings of the Gospels, while others were new. We are not at present concerned with the many questions which were thus raised (see p. 128 ff.), but the importance of the discovery was undeniable, especially when it was followed next day by the finding of another uncial fragment containing the greater part of the first chapter of St. Matthew's Gospel, written not later than the third century, and therefore a century older than the oldest manuscript of the New Testament previously known (see p. 115 f.). Both leaves, Dr. Grenfell suggests, may not improbably form "the remains of a library belonging to some Christian who perished in the persecution during Diocletian's reign, and whose books were then thrown away." [9]

Along with these, and other almost equally sensational finds, Oxyrhynchus yielded an enormous mass of documents of the most miscellaneous character dating from the Roman Conquest of Egypt to the tenth century after Christ, when papyrus was superseded by paper as a writing material.

Publication of Papyri.—Of these, thanks to the unwearied energy of the discoverers, upwards of eighteen hundred texts have now been published in fifteen volumes of *Oxyrhynchus Papyri*, issued under the auspices of the Graeco-Roman Branch of the Egypt Exploration Society. It will require, so the editors inform me, at least the same number of additional volumes to complete the publication of the Oxyrhynchus collection alone.

Other large volumes contain the results of the same editors' work on the collection of papyri formed by the late Lord Amherst, and on their own discoveries in the Fayûm district, at Hibeh, and at Tebtunis. The finds at the last named spot were of a novel character. In the course of their excavations the Oxford scholars came across a large cemetery of crocodile-mummies, and one of their workmen, disgusted at finding crocodiles where he had been expecting sarcophagi, smashed one of them in pieces, only to disclose the surprising fact that the creature was wrapped in sheets of papyrus, and that in various instances papyrus rolls had been stuffed into the throat or other cavities of the crocodile mummies.[10] As might have been expected from the circumstances, few literary texts were found amongst these papyri, but, on the other hand, they included many important official documents, often of great size, furnishing valuable information as to the internal administration of Egypt under the later Ptolemies.

Apart from the publications associated with the names of Dr. Grenfell and Dr. Hunt, of which only the more important have been named, this country can boast of three volumes of *Flinders Petrie Papyri*, edited by the late Sir John P. Mahaffy, latterly with the assistance of Dr. J. G. Smyly, to which reference has already been made, and five stately volumes of the *Catalogue of Greek Papyri in the British Museum*, edited by Sir F. G. Kenyon and Dr. H. I. Bell. To Dr. Hunt's volume of literary texts from the *Greek Papyri in the John Rylands Library*, Manchester, there has also been added a second volume containing nearly four hundred texts of a most varied character, in the preparation of which Mr. J. de M. Johnson of Oxford, and Mr. V. Martin of Geneva, have taken a leading part.

Of collections published abroad, in addition to the older Turin (1826-7), Leyden (1843-85), and Paris (1865) Papyri, we have four large volumes of texts from the Berlin Museum, the result of the collaboration of many scholars, and a beginning has recently been made with a fifth volume. Smaller, though hardly less noteworthy, publications are associated with Vienna, Leipzig, Strassburg, Florence, Geneva, Lille, Hamburg, Munich, and various other places. America is represented by various groups of papyri published under the editorship of Professor E. J. Goodspeed of Chicago, who also assisted in Part ii. of the already mentioned *Tebtunis Papyri*.[11]

The general result is that there are now available about ten thousand published documents, and that these will be largely added to as soon as normal literary activities are resumed. Whether the still unedited papyri have any great surprises in store for us, it is vain even to conjecture. But even if they have not, they will serve a useful purpose in illustrating and confirming the lexical and other results that have already been reached, and of increasing still further our stock of first hand documentary evidence regarding the most important period in the world's history.

Classification of Papyri.—The papyri are generally classified under the two main heads Literary and Non-Literary, with the Biblical and Theological texts occupying a position about midway between the two.

Literary.—Of the strictly literary or classical texts about a thousand have now been published, of which it is estimated that about one-third are Homeric, that rather less than one-third contain texts of the works of other ancient writers already known to us, and that rather more than a third contain new writings, or writings which, though known by name, were believed to have been hopelessly lost. Amongst these last we may specially mention, in addition to those already referred to, a papyrus roll containing several of the orations of Lysias—a fragment of an historian variously identified with Ephorus, Theopompus, or Cratippus, which deals with the history of Greece in the years 396 and 395 B.C.—portions of five of the hundred plays of Menander which, after long enjoying great popularity, had for some reason almost totally disappeared—a sufficient number of fragments of the *Hypsipyle* of Euripides to admit of the reconstruction of the plot—a number of Sappho's songs—and a long and valuable manuscript from the first half of the second century containing parts of a number of the *Paeans* of Pindar.[12]

Any discussion of these classical texts does not fall within our scope, but, apart from their general interest, covering as they do so many and varied branches of Greek literature, it may be asked whether the new manuscripts of extant works, going back to a date earlier by many hundreds of years than the great mass of Greek classical manuscripts, have any special light to throw on questions of text, and more particularly on the conjectures which from time to time have been brought forward for the amendment of the received text. The latter point has been specially investigated by Sir F. G. Kenyon in an address delivered before the British Academy in 1904, and is also referred to by the same writer in an article on "Greek Papyri and Recent Discoveries," which appeared in the *Quarterly Review* for April, 1908, where (p. 343) the general conclusion is reached "that the tradition of the classical texts is substantially sound, and that the best vellum MSS. of the tenth and later centuries are as good as, and often better than, the Egyptian papyri of a thousand years earlier."[13]

At first sight, therefore, we may not seem to have gained much in this particular from the new discoveries, and yet surely the confirmation of our traditional text from such ancient witnesses counts for a great deal, to say nothing of the romantic way in which that confirmation has come.

Nor must we forget the interesting testimony which these remnants bear to the great popularity of Greek letters even in such a provincial town as Oxyrhynchus. " It is not," says Professor Hunt, " till the Byzantine period that a marked decline becomes apparent, to be traced partly to the material decay which was beginning to make its effects generally felt, partly also, I think, to the spread of Christianity. A new literature had come into favour, and though the great classics were still in wide circulation—Homer, Demosthenes and Menander being prominent—the range tended to become more and more restricted. The right-minded man would tend to replace Sappho with the Psalms, and satisfy his appetite for history and romance with lives of the saints and martyrs."[14]

Biblical and Theological.—In these circumstances, it is perhaps to be wondered at that the number of Biblical and Theological texts recovered is not larger. We might have expected, for example, in view of the close connexion of the Septuagint, or Greek version of the Old Testament, with Egypt, that very considerable portions of it would have been found, whereas the recovered fragments do not number more than twenty-five or thirty in all, and only one contains a passage of any considerable length. But they are again at least sufficient to test the general accuracy of what has been ordinarily regarded as the best text, and are regularly cited by the editors in the critical apparatus of the larger Cambridge Septuagint.[15]

The same applies to our New Testament fragments. Of these I was able to describe twenty-three in my *New Testament Documents* published in 1913, and at least eleven can now be added to the list. More detailed reference must be reserved for a subsequent chapter (see Chapter V.), but when we remember that the list includes at least six texts belonging to the third century, that the papyri as a whole are drawn from twelve of our New Testament books, that the longest of them, dating from the first half of the fourth century, contains about one-third of the Epistle to the Hebrews, including the later chapters which are wanting in the Vatican Codex, and that, so far as they go, they confirm generally the type of text found in that Codex and its allies, it is clear that they cannot lightly be set aside.

Another opportunity will be found of dealing with other classes of Christian documents of papyrus, and of illustrating the light which they throw on the early history and worship of the Church (see Chapter V.), but in the meantime it is necessary to refer to the great mass of non-literary documents, which can be numbered not by hundreds but by thousands.

Non-literary.—The contents of these non-literary documents, as has already been stated, are of the most miscellaneous character, comprising as they do all manner of official documents such as Imperial rescripts, accounts of judicial proceedings, tax and census papers, contracts of marriage and divorce, notices of birth and death, and so forth, along with a large number of private letters touching upon all sides of family and everyday life.[16]

And as thus the contents of these documents are wide as life itself, so they supply materials for the most varied fields of human learning. Their value to the historian and the jurist is apparent on the surface, while with their aid the geographer can reconstruct the map of ancient Egypt with a precision previously impossible. To the palaeographer again, who was previously sadly hampered by want of actual evidence for judging the development of ordinary script, they offer an uninterrupted series of examples, many of them exactly dated by year and month and day, from the third century before Christ to the eighth century after Christ. And to the philologist they show the true place of the Koinē (Κοινή), the common Greek of the period, as distinguished from the dialects of the classical period, in the development of the Greek language. Examples of the Koinē on its literary side had not, indeed, been previously wanting, but now, for the first time, it was possible to see it in undress, as it was spoken and written by the ordinary men and women of the day.

It was from this last point of view that the importance of the papyri for the Biblical student was first realized, for it was now made evident that the so-called " peculiarities " of Biblical Greek, apart from those due to the influence of translation Greek, and to the moulding power of Christianity, were in reality no " peculiarities " at all, but arose from the fact that the New Testament writers made use for the most part of the common speech of their day. The Book, that is, which was specially intended for the people was written in a tongue " understanded by the people."

If the papyri had done nothing else than make this clear, it would have been worth all the labour that has been bestowed upon them ;

but their significance, even from the linguistic point of view alone, is far from being exhausted by any such general statement. Not only do they confirm the traditional meaning of words which had hitherto rested on very insufficient evidence, but in not a few instances they have supplied new meanings by which difficult and obscure passages have been rendered intelligible. And above all they have added fresh reality to much familiar Biblical phraseology by lifting it back once more into direct contact with the actual life and thought of the day.

It is only by actual illustration, to which we shall turn in succeeding chapters, that these and similar gains from the papyri can be made clear. But enough I trust has been said to show how great is the debt of gratitude under which we rest to the original discoverers and interpreters of these fascinating texts, and what a wide and fruitful field of study they offer to all who are willing to devote themselves to it.

The Papyri and the Original New Testament Writings

New Testament Autographs.—In the preceding chapter I sketched briefly the history of papyrus discovery, and indicated the bearing of the new finds upon various departments of human knowledge, laying special emphasis upon the light which they throw upon the language of our New Testament documents. Before, however, we turn to examine and illustrate in detail the nature of that light, it may be well to ask whether the papyri have anything to teach us regarding the outward appearance and form of the original New Testament writings. We have become so accustomed to think of the New Testament as a single printed volume, with its contents arranged in a certain fixed order, and with every appliance for quick and easy reference, that we lose sight of the first stage of its history, when it circulated not as one book but as many books, possessed of varying degrees of authority, and not yet invested with the full sacred character which they afterwards enjoyed.

Outward Appearance.—To begin then with the outward appearance of the New Testament autographs, there can be little doubt that they were written in the first instance on separate papyrus rolls, which would vary in size according to the length of the books. A short Epistle, for example, like the Second Epistle to the Thessalonians, would form a roll of about fifteen inches in length with the contents arranged in some five columns, while St. Paul's longest Epistle, the Epistle to the Romans, would run to about eleven feet and a half. The shortest of the Gospels, St. Mark's, would occupy about nineteen feet; the longest, St. Luke's, about thirty-one or thirty-two feet. And the Apocalypse of St. John has been estimated at fifteen feet. Taking the other books on the same scale, Sir F. G. Kenyon, to whom the foregoing figures are also due, has calculated that if the whole New Testament was written out in order on a single roll, the roll would extend to more than two hundred feet in length, obviously an utterly unworkable size.[1] This alone makes it clear that not until the papyrus stage in their history was past, and use was made of both sides of parchment or vellum leaves, was it possible to include all the books of the New Testament in a single volume.

If then we wish to picture to ourselves what a Pauline Epistle or Letter, say the Epistle to the Galatians, looked like, when it first left the Apostle's hands, we must think of a roll of papyrus, covered over on the inside with Greek writing in parallel columns. The margins between the columns would for the most part be narrow; but there would be blank spaces at the top and bottom of the roll capable of receiving any additions or corrections which the scribe might wish to make.

Addresses.—The roll, when finished, would be rolled up much as we roll up a map, and fastened together with a string, sealing as a rule being reserved for official and legal documents. The address would be written on the back or outside of the roll, and, unlike the long addresses or titles to which we have become accustomed, which belong to a much later period in the history of the New Testament, it would be in the fewest possible words—" To Galatians," " To Romans," " To Hebrews," and so forth. More was unnecessary, for the actual delivery of the letters would be entrusted to special Christian messengers or couriers. The post of the time was an Imperial post, organized for the transmission of Government dispatches and messages,[2] and ordinary correspondents had to rely upon the help of some friend or passing stranger to carry their letters for them. In the case of the New Testament Letters, this had the advantage of allowing their writers to supplement their contents with verbal messages. On the other hand, it is owing to the very brevity of the original addresses that many of the questions which have greatly exercised scholars have arisen.

What, for example, was the country of the

Galatians, to whom the Epistle known by that name was addressed ? Was it, as Bishop Lightfoot used to tell us, in Northern Galatia, the comparatively small district of that name, occupied by the Gauls ? Or was it, as Sir William M. Ramsay maintains, in Southern Galatia, the territory included in the Roman province of the name, and comprising the towns of Derbe, Lystra, Iconium and Pisidian Antioch ? This is not the place to bring forward the arguments on the one side or the other. All that we are concerned with is that, if the address had been fuller from the first, and had been transmitted to us along with the rest of the Epistle, there would have been no occasion for arguments at all.

The same is true of the destination of the Epistle to the Hebrews, which has been variously found in such places as Jerusalem, Alexandria, or Rome. Fortunately, interesting though these questions are, our inability to answer them so definitely as we would like does not detract from the value of the Letters in themselves, or obscure the present-day significance of their message.

Letters or Epistles.—I have been referring to Letters rather than to Epistles, and I have done so of set purpose, because the former title helps to emphasize the direct, personal character of the writings of which we are thinking. The distinction must, of course, not be overpressed.[3] There are wide differences between the Pauline Letters themselves, as notably between the great Epistle to the Romans, which amounts almost to a theological treatise, and the unstudied art of the little note to Philemon, while even this last, in virtue of its writer and his subject, is on a wholly different plane from an ordinary papyrus letter. At the same time nothing helps us more to grasp the reality of the message in the Pauline writings than to remember that these writings are popular rather than literary in their origin, and were intended, in the first instance, not for publication, or for after-ages, but to meet the immediate practical needs of the Churches and individuals to whom they were in the first instance addressed. As Sir William M. Ramsay puts it, " In the individual case they

The Papyri and New Testament Writings

discover the universal principle, and state it in such a way as to reach the heart of every man similarly situated, and yet they state this, not in the way of formal exposition, but in the way of direct personal converse, written in place of spoken." [4]

This comes out very clearly in the more formal parts of the Pauline writings, the opening addresses and the closing salutations, which follow the conventional epistolary forms of the time.

To take an example. Here is a private letter from Oxyrhynchus, written in 16 A.D., in which a certain Theon recommended the bearer of the letter, Hermophilus, to the notice of his brother Heraclides, who acted as royal scribe of the district. The letter may, therefore, be compared with the "letters of commendation" (συστατικαὶ ἐπιστολαί), to which St. Paul refers in 2 Cor. iii. 1. I give it in Grenfell and Hunt's translation.

> Theon to Heraclides his brother, many greetings and wishes for good health. Hermophilus the bearer of this letter is (the friend or relative) of .... erius, and asked me to write to you. Her-

mophilus declares that he has business at Kerkemounis. Please therefore further him in this matter, as is just. For the rest take care of yourself that you may remain in good health. Good-bye. The 3rd year of Tiberius Caesar Augustus, Phaophi 3.

On the *verso* or back is the address—

To Heraclides, basilicogrammateus of the Oxyrhynchite and Cynopolite nomes.[5]

The writer's name, you will notice, comes first: then the name of the person to whom the letter is addressed: and then the greeting which the former sends to the latter—all just as in the letter which Claudius Lysias sends to Felix in Acts xxiii. 26 (cf. 1 Thess. i. 1, *al.*). Similarly Theon's letter is closed with a parting greeting, "Good-bye," in the same way that St. Paul is careful to append to his letters some such wish as "The grace of our Lord Jesus Christ be with you" (1 Thess. v. 28; cf. 2 Thess. iii. 18, *al.*).

Or to take another example, which, in addition to the more formal resemblances already noted, lets us see in an ordinary letter the "prayer" and the "thanksgiving," which are such characteristic marks of Paul's attitude towards those whom he is addressing. The letter, which is from the Fayûm district, is addressed by a mother to her children, and belongs to the end of the second or the beginning of the third century A.D.

> Serapias to her children Ptolemaeus and Apolinaria and Ptolemaeus heartiest greeting. Above all I pray that you may be in health, which is for me the most necessary of all things. I make my obeisance to the lord Serapis, praying that I may receive word that you are in health, even as I pray for your general welfare. I rejoiced when I received letters that you were well recovered. Salute Ammonous with his children and wife and those who love you. Cyrilla saluteth you, and Hermias the daughter of Hermias, Hermanoubis the nurse, Athenais the teacher (?), Cyrilla, Casia ... Empis, in fact all who are here. Please therefore write me what you are about, for you know that, if I receive your letters, I am glad on account of your well-being. I pray that you may prosper.

On the *verso* the letter has two addresses, one in the original hand to the effect—

> Deliver to Ptolemaeus my child. Salute ...

And the second in a different hand—

> Deliver to Ptolemaeus the brother of Apolinaria.

From this it would appear that the first recipient of the letter was Ptolemaeus, and that afterwards he readdressed it to his brother of the same name.[6]

Apart altogether from its general structure, the letter will recall to every careful reader various phrases, which in closely similar terms occur again and again in St. Paul's letters, to say nothing of the long list of closing salutations, such as meet us at the end of the Epistle to the Romans.

The same general features appear in the only other letter we can cite at present. It is a family letter written by a soldier-son to his father in the second century A.D. The boy had gone with his regiment to Italy, and he writes to announce his safe arrival after a stormy passage, and to let his father know what he is about.

> Apion to Epimachus his father and lord, heartiest greetings. First of all I pray that you are in health and continually prosper and fare well with my sister and her daughter and my brother. I thank the lord Serapis that when I was in danger at sea he saved me. Straightway when I entered Misenum I received my travelling

money from Caesar, three gold pieces. And I am
well. I beg you, therefore, my lord father, write
me a few lines, first regarding your health,
secondly regarding that of my brother and sister,
thirdly that I may kiss your hand, because you
have brought me up well, and on this account I
hope to be quickly promoted, if the gods will.
Give many greetings to Capito, and to my brother
and sister, and to Serenilla, and my friends. I
send you a little portrait of myself at the hands
of Euctemon. And my (military) name is
Antonius Maximus. I pray for your good health.

The address on the back runs :

> To Philadelphia for Epim X achus from Apion
> his son.

And to this, two lines running in the opposite direction have been added to the effect that the letter is to be conveyed by military post.[7]

In the simple construction of the sentences and the general absence of connecting particles, the letter is a good illustration of the epistolary style of the period ; but what we are more immediately concerned with at present is the general mould or form in which it is cast. It begins with a greeting. This is followed by a prayer for his father's health and prosperity, and this by a thanksgiving for the deliverance the writer has himself experienced. Then comes the main body of the letter, containing the special news he desires to send his father. Then a number of salutations to various friends, and finally a closing prayer or valediction. Greeting, Prayer, Thanksgiving, General Contents, Salutations, and Closing Valediction—these then formed the framework of an ordinary letter of St. Paul's time, and that framework, with necessary modifications, the Apostle followed in his letters, as anyone can verify for himself.

This fact can hardly fail to bring these letters nearer to us, and emphasize the personal background which underlies them. We learn with a definiteness, which perhaps we did not feel before, that the Apostle was sending a living message to living men and women. And the more clearly we are able to discover exactly what that message meant for them, the better are we prepared to realize what it is still intended to teach us.[8]

Dictation.—St. Paul's adoption of the ordinary epistolary practice of his time can also be illustrated by his use of dictation. We are accustomed, perhaps, to think of dictation as a comparatively modern practice, but the papyri show that it was well established at the beginning of the Christian Era, and even then there is every reason to believe that it had already a long history behind it. Constantly at the end of a papyrus letter we find a docket to the effect that it was written by So-and-so on behalf of So-and-so, because he or she " did not know letters," or was too " unlettered " to write for himself or herself.[9] In other cases the phrase is varied, and the use of a scribe is put down to the fact that the author of the letter could only write " slowly " ($\beta\rho\alpha\delta\acute{\epsilon}\omega\varsigma$).

A good example is afforded by a papyrus of 16 A.D., in which Ptolemaeus, who describes himself as " superintendent of the donkeys of Apollonius son of Alexander," acknowledges receipt of a thousand bundles of hay. After the form has been made out, a note is added to the effect:

> Marion his secretary wrote for him because he writes slowly.

And then Ptolemaeus appends his own signature in rude capital letters to authenticate the whole :

I Ptolemaeus have received.[10]

It is, of course, perfectly true that St. Paul stood on a different footing. As an educated man, he could easily have written out his letters with his own hand, and no doubt on occasions did so (cf. p. 41 f.). At the same time we can easily understand what a relief it would be to him in the midst of his daily toil and pressure to get the assistance of a disciple or friend in the actual work of writing. And that he did make use of such aid is borne out by the evidence of some of the letters themselves. Tertius's postscript in Rom. xvi. 22, "I Tertius, who write the letter, salute you in the Lord," can hardly be understood otherwise than that his hand had actually penned the Apostolic message. And the manner of St. Paul's reference to his authenticating signature in 2 Thess. iii. 17, 18, " The salutation of me Paul with mine own hand, which is the token in every letter : so I write. The grace of our

Lord Jesus Christ be with you all," is such as to imply that the body of the letter had been written by some one else (cf. 1 Cor. xvi. 21 ff., Col. iv. 18).

When, then, we think of St. Paul at work on one of his letters, we can imagine him pacing up and down his little room, his thoughts, his eyes, fixed on distant Corinth or Philippi, and, as the needs of his correspondents rise up before him, pouring forth his glowing sentences to the scribe sitting at his feet. And then, when the scribe's work is done, revising what he has written, and adding his authenticating signature " with mine own hand Paul," to show that in reality the whole letter comes from him.

The Epistle to the Galatians is particularly interesting in this connexion. In the case of this very severe letter, it is possible that St. Paul may not have employed an amanuensis at all. Where there was so much to condemn, St. Paul, with that innate courtesy which was so natural to him, and which reveals at every hand Paul the gentleman, would not like the idea of any one coming between him and those erring but loved " brethren." And accordingly he may have dispensed with the usual assistance, and written the whole letter with his own hand. In any case, he is careful to emphasize his personal part in the closing paragraph. " See "—so he introduces it— " with what large letters ($\pi\eta\lambda\iota\kappa o\iota s$ $\gamma\rho\alpha\mu\mu\alpha\sigma\iota\nu$) I write unto you with mine own hand " (ch. vi. 11).

I have been inclined sometimes to see in the " large letters " the rough, sprawling characters of a man unaccustomed to much writing, or whose hand of writ had suffered from the use of his hands in daily toil. But it is more likely that, as in inscriptions and elsewhere, the " large letters " were used for emphasis, to draw special attention to what followed. The very dangers to which the faith of the Galatian converts was exposed made it the more necessary that they should be assured in unmistakable terms of the new life open to all through the Cross of Christ with its accompanying " peace " and " mercy," and so be prepared for the Apostle's characteristic and comprehensive salutation : " The grace of our Lord Jesus Christ be with your spirit, brethren " (Gal. vi. 18, R.V.).[11]

To return, however, to the practice of dictation. Apart altogether from its more personal aspects, the general use of dictation is of significance as helping us to understand the vigour and directness of St. Paul's style. His letters are speeches, spoken aloud and intended to be read aloud to the Churches to whom they were addressed (see *e.g.* 1 Thess. v. 27—ἀναγνωσθῆναι). Nor is this all, but have we not also here at least a partial explanation of the long involved sentences and the broken grammar by which they are so often distinguished ? Had St. Paul been committing his thoughts with his own hand to paper, the very act of writing would have restrained him. But in dictating he was freer to let himself go, to pile up clause upon clause, until it sometimes seems as if he were never to get to the end of his sentences (*e.g.* Eph. i. 3-14, 15-23), to break off at a word, or even to interject a qualifying statement to correct something he had just said (*e.g.* 1 Cor. i. 16 f.).

There is still another point in this connexion which may be noted. May not the employment of different amanuenses help to explain the differences of vocabulary and style in the letters, which have sometimes been urged against their authenticity? These differences no doubt are attributable to many and varied causes, such as the changes in the Apostle's surroundings, in the nature of the message he is delivering, and even in his own spiritual growth and apprehension. But is it not also possible that in some cases St. Paul left greater freedom to his scribes than in others? One letter might be dictated almost word for word. In another the Apostle might be content to indicate in general terms what he wished to be said, and then leave it to his scribe to put the message into words.

For this latter possibility an interesting parallel may be cited from the mission-field. When a European missionary in China wishes to send a message, he first writes it down in his own Chinese, and then submits it to a "writer," who drafts it afresh into the correct classical phraseology. After revision it is sent out by the missionary " as his own authentic message."[12]

To many it may seem, however, that such procedure would minimize too much the Apostle's personal share in the production of his letters, and where we have no definite data to go upon, we must be careful not to give too free rein to imagination, however useful that faculty may be in the interpretation of an historical document. And the same may be said of the conjecture—and here it is only a conjecture—that the New Testament scribes made use of some form of shorthand.

Shorthand.—I cannot attempt here to trace the history of the use of shorthand. It must be enough that some such form of writing was undoubtedly in use at the beginning of the Christian Era.[13] The question is complicated by the fact that the name is sometimes given to what may well have been only an abbreviated or contracted form of writing. On the other hand, we have undoubted instances of the use of tachygraphic signs or symbols in the papyri, though hitherto no key has been found to their interpretation. And, what is more to the point, we are now in possession amongst the Oxyrhynchus papyri of a very interesting contract belonging to the year 155 A.D., in which an ex-magistrate of Oxyrhynchus apprentices his slave to a shorthand writer (σημιογράφῳ) for two years to be taught to read and write shorthand. The teacher is to receive 120 drachmae in all by way of payment, of which he has already received a first instalment of 40 drachmae. But the second instalment is not to be paid until the boy has learned the whole system, and the third only when he " writes fluently in every respect and reads faultlessly " (ἐκ παντὸς λόγου πεζοῦ γράφοντος καὶ ἀναγεινώσ[κον]τος ἀμέμπτως).[14]

It would not, therefore, be out of keeping with the practice of the time for the Apostolic scribes to have made use of some such method. But, as stated above, we can only hint at a possibility, remembering further that an art, which was practised by regularly trained official scribes, may well have been wholly beyond the reach of the humble friends and dependents, on whose assistance St.

Paul and the other New Testament writers relied.

The main thing, after all, is that whatever stages the Pauline letters may have passed through in the act of composition, they come to us as the Apostle's, bearing in every line the unmistakable stamp of his genius, and authenticated by his autograph. Sometimes, as we have already seen, St. Paul expressly tells us that he finished off his letters with his own hand (cf. p. 40 f.), but in other cases he would seem to have been content to add his closing greeting, without mentioning himself, trusting that the writing would be recognized as his—a practice for which again the papyri furnish ample warrant.

Method of Reading.—We have not done yet with the light which their original papyrus form throws upon our New Testament books. The roll-form determines the manner in which their contents were read. Holding the roll in his left hand, the reader gradually unrolled it with his right, and then, as he followed it column by column, he rolled up with his left hand what he had already read. As the contents would be written continuously without division into the chapters or the verses, to which we have become so accustomed, it is obvious that subsequent reference to particular passages would be by no means easy.

This has again a significant bearing upon certain facts in the history of the different books. Let us notice two points. The first is of a somewhat general character.

Those who have studied what is known as the Synoptic Problem are aware that there is wide-spread agreement amongst scholars that our present Synoptic Gospels are formed upon the basis of older written documents, and further that these written documents have often been used with a degree of freedom which, with our modern literary canons, we would hardly have expected. And the explanation, as Dr. Sanday has shown in his illuminating Essay on " The Conditions under which the Gospels were written in their Bearing upon some Difficulties of the Synoptic Problem," [16] is to be sought in the different procedure of the modern and the ancient copyist. The former would have the document he was using constantly spread out before him, and there would be little or no interval of time between the reading of its text and the reproduction; whereas the latter "would not have his copy before him, but would consult it from time to time. He would not follow it clause by clause and phrase by phrase, but would probably read through a whole paragraph at once, and trust to his memory to carry the substance of it safely from the one book to the other" (p. 18), or, as we would rather say in the present connexion, "from the original roll to the copy he was making."

And so again with the general looseness of quotation from the New Testament writings in early Christian literature. How could it be otherwise when we remember the fewness of the copies of these writings which were at first in circulation, and the length of time it would take to discover in a closely written roll the exact passage which the writer wished to cite! The marvel, indeed, is not the changes which were introduced into the quotations, but the general accuracy with which they were reproduced.

Questions of Structure.—Something will be said in a concluding chapter of the bearing of the papyrus period upon the grave question of textual corruption; but meanwhile we may conclude our present survey by asking whether that period has any light to throw upon various questions of structure which have been much discussed in connexion with certain of the New Testament books.

In a papyrus roll the opening and closing leaves would naturally be those most handled, and consequently those most likely to be mutilated or broken off. Is it possible that we have here an explanation of a well-known difficulty in connexion with the closing chapter of St. Mark's Gospel. In that chapter, as you will see from the marginal note in the Revised Version, *vv.* 9-20 are wanting in our two principal Greek manuscripts, the Gospel in them ending with the last words of *v.* 8, "for they were afraid" (ἐφοβοῦντο γάρ). That this was the original ending of the Gospel is, on various grounds into which we need not enter at present, most unlikely. And it is at least a happy conjecture that in an early copy (the only one for the time being in circulation) the last leaf had been lost, and that consequently in copies made from it the Gospel came to the same abrupt ending. This mutilated manuscript could not, however, long satisfy the mind of the Church, and consequently new endings were added to round off the narrative, one of these being the ending with which we are familiar in our ordinary New Testament text.[17]

Or, to take another example, this time of addition, not of loss. Questions have been raised in connexion with what is now the closing chapter of the Epistle to the Romans. There is, for one thing, a certain amount of textual confusion regarding the position of the various benedictions and doxologies towards the close of the Epistle, while, as regards matter, it is on the face of it strange that St. Paul should have been sending so many personal greetings to a Church he had not founded, nor even at this time personally visited, and with whose members, therefore, he could hardly be expected to be intimate. What if this last chapter was originally a separate, short letter—addressed perhaps to the Church of Ephesus—which, from being preserved in the same *capsa* or box as the letter to the Romans, came afterwards to be copied out along with it.

Once more, careful readers of the Second Epistle to the Corinthians can hardly fail to have been struck with the sudden change of tone in the four concluding chapters. In the earlier chapters (i.-ix.) the Apostle has found much to commend in his Corinthian converts, and then suddenly, when we are least expecting it, he passes into severe rebuke and reproach. Can it be that fresh news of a disquieting nature has reached St. Paul, just as he finished Chap. ix. ? Or may it be that the last four chapters are in reality no part of the Epistle to which they are now attached ? In 2 Cor. vii. 8 the Apostle himself refers to a severe Epistle, which has generally been regarded as lost. What if we are to find it, in whole or in part, in these four chapters, which some early copyist may have attached at the end of the roll containing Chaps. i.-ix., because they were addressed to the same Church.

The question must of course be decided on wider grounds than we can bring forward here, and there is much to be said on both sides. The only point we are at present concerned with is that the method of roll production and of roll circulation, as distinguished from the ordinary book form, does not make such a theory impossible. It is, indeed, by no means uncommon during the papyrus period to find documents fastened together to form a single roll, and an example is also forthcoming of a collection of private letters, in which a later letter is placed before one written earlier, perhaps, however, because it had been received earlier.[18]

Papyrus Codex.—To prevent misconception, we must add that the papyrus roll stage of our New Testament writings was of comparatively short duration, the papyrus roll giving place to the papyrus codex, that is to papyrus leaves, not fastened together in a roll, but placed one upon the top of the other in codex or book form. When exactly this transition took place, it is impossible to say, but it must have been at a comparatively early date. For while classical writings continued for long to be circulated in rolls, the codex seems to have been regarded as specially suitable for Christian writings. Most of our earliest New Testament Texts on papyrus are, as we shall see later (cf. p. 115 ff.), fragmentary leaves from codices, and the same thing applies to the first discovered Sayings of Jesus, and to many other ancient Christian documents.

The point is of some importance, as it enables us to trace the gradual progression of our New Testament documents from the papyrus roll to the papyrus codex, and then from the papyrus codex to the parchment or vellum codex, which meets us in the great uncial manuscripts of the fourth and succeeding centuries.

"Common" Greek and the New Testament

WE have seen something of the light which the papyri throw upon the outward appearance of the original New Testament documents, and upon the manner in which they were first written and circulated. We pass to another point of still greater practical importance, and that is the nature of the language made use of by their writers.

"New Testament" Greek.—That language was of course Greek. Attempts indeed have been made to show that behind the Greek dress in which our New Testament books have come down to us there were in certain cases Aramaic originals.[1] But, even if this were established, it does not alter the fact that it is in Greek they were first generally circulated, and in Greek that we have learned to know them. The exact character of the Greek thus employed has, however, proved a matter of eager discussion. No one can read the Greek New Testament without realizing that both in vocabulary and grammar it differs very considerably from what is commonly described as Classical Greek, or the Greek used in the most brilliant period of the literary history of Greece, and in consequence it has frequently been urged that it forms a language by itself, which may be fittingly described as " New Testament " Greek.

Various Explanations.—Various explanations have been offered as to how this Greek may have arisen, one of the commonest being that it was " Judaic " or " Hebraic " Greek, due to the fact that its writers, as Jews (with the probable exception of St. Luke), used it as foreigners, and further had, in most cases, been nurtured on the translation Greek of the Septuagint, or Greek Version of the Old Testament.

Now there can be no doubt that their Jewish upbringing would inevitably influence the language of the New Testament writers, and that it is vain to deny the presence of so-called Aramaisms and Hebraisms in the New Testament. However much these may have been over-emphasized in the past, they were in themselves inevitable, " birthmarks " of the writer's origin, just as his native Gaelic can generally be traced behind a Highlander's English.

Its real Character.—But while this is so, the explanation of the real character of so-called New Testament Greek is much more interesting, and for it we have in the first instance to thank the German scholar, Adolf Deissmann, now Professor of New Testament Exegesis in the University of Berlin. While still a pastor at Marburg, Dr. (then Mr.) Deissmann happened one day to be turning over in the University Library at Heidelberg a new section of a volume containing transcripts from the collection of Greek Papyri at Berlin. And as he read, he was suddenly struck by the likeness of the language of these papyri to the language with which he was familiar in his study of the Greek New Testament. Further study deepened in his mind the extent of this likeness, and he realized that he held in his hand the real key to the old problem.

So far from the Greek of the New Testament being a language by itself, or even, as one German scholar called it, " a language of the Holy Ghost,"[2] its main feature was that it was the ordinary vernacular Greek of the period, not the language of contemporary literature, which was often influenced by an attempt to imitate the great authors of classical times, but the language of everyday life, as it was spoken and written by the ordinary men and women of the day, or, as it is often described, the Koinē or " Common " Greek of the great Graeco-Roman world.[3]

That, then, is Deissmann's general conclusion, which quickly found an enthusiastic and brilliant advocate in this country in the person of Dr. J. H. Moulton. And though the zeal of the first discoverers of the new light may have sometimes led them to go rather far in ignoring the Semitisms, on the one hand, and the literary culture of the New Testament writers, on the other, their main conclusion has found general acceptance, and we have come to realize with a definiteness unknown before that the book intended for the people was written in the people's own tongue.

Anticipations of this View.—It is somewhat strange that this discovery was so long in being made. Publications of papyri, which furnish the principal evidence in support of it, go back as far as 1826, but there is nothing to show that this particular way of utilizing their discoveries ever occurred to the first editors. At the same time it is interesting to notice various anticipations from other sources of what such discoveries might mean, or, as it has been called, of Deissmannism before Deissmann.

In the *Prolegomena* to his translation of Winer's well-known *Grammar of New Testament Greek*, published in 1859, Professor Masson, at one time Professor in the University of Athens, writes: " The diction of the New Testament is the plain and unaffected Hellenic of the Apostolic Age, as employed by Greek-speaking Christians when discoursing on religious subjects. . . . Perfectly natural and unaffected, it is free from all tinge of vulgarity on the one hand, and from every trace of studied finery on the other. Apart from the Hebraisms—the number of which has, for the most part, been grossly exaggerated—the New Testament may be considered as exhibiting the only genuine *facsimile* of the colloquial diction employed by *unsophisticated* Grecian gentlemen of the first century, who spoke without pedantry—as ἰδιῶται (' private persons '), and not as σοφισταί (' adepts ') " (p. viii. f.).[4]

A second testimony to much the same effect will be found in the article " Greek Language (Biblical)," contributed by Mr. (afterwards Principal Sir James) Donaldson to the third edition of Kitto's *Cyclopaedia of Biblical Literature*, edited by Dr. W. Lindsay Alexander (Edinburgh, 1862-66). There, in Vol. ii. p. 170[a], the writer states : " Now it seems to us that the language used by the Septuagint and N(ew) T(estament) writers was the language used in common conversation, learned by them, not through books, but most likely in childhood from household talk, or, if not, through subsequent oral instruction. If this be the case, then the Septuagint is the first translation which was made for the great masses of the people in their own language, and the N(ew) T(estament) writers are the first to appeal to men through the common vulgar language intelligible to all who spoke Greek. The common Greek thus used is indeed considerably modified by the circumstances of the writers, but these modifications no more turn the Greek into a peculiar dialect than do Americanisms or Scotticisms turn the English of Americans and Scotsmen into peculiar dialects of English."[5]

Still more interesting is the prophecy ascribed to Professor (afterwards Bishop) J. B. Lightfoot in the previous year, 1863. Lecturing to his class at Cambridge, Dr. Lightfoot is reported to have said: "You are not to suppose that the word [some New Testament word which had its only classical authority in Herodotus] had fallen out of use in the interval, only that it had not been used in the books which remain to us : probably it had been part of the common speech all along. I will go further, and say that if we could only recover letters that ordinary people wrote to each other without any thought of being literary, we should have the greatest possible help for the understanding of the language of the New Testament generally."[6]

The significance of this quotation is unmistakable, and it is followed, twenty-one years later, by what is, so far as I know, the first definite mention in this country of the papyri in connexion with New Testament study. It occurs in Dean Farrar's well-known volume, *The Messages of the Books* (London, Macmillan, 1884), where, in a footnote to his chapter on the " Form of the New Testament Epistles," the writer remarks : " It is an interesting subject of inquiry to what extent there was at this period an ordinary form of correspondence which (as amongst ourselves) was to some extent fixed. In the papyrus rolls of the British Museum (edited for the trustees by J. Forshall [in 1839]) there are forms and phrases which constantly remind us of St. Paul " (p. 151).

New Gains.—The hint, thus thrown out, was unfortunately not followed up at the time, but if the full significance of the papyri for the

New Testament student was long in being recognized, no one can complain of lack of attention to the subject at the present day. It is leading to the re-writing of our Lexicons and Grammars of the New Testament, and no modern Commentary on any of its books fails to avail itself of the help afforded by these new treasures from Egypt. That help is very varied.

Vocabulary.—For one thing, the papyri greatly reduce the number of words which the Lexicons were in the habit of describing as found only in Biblical or Ecclesiastical Greek. These used to be reckoned at about five hundred, but now, thanks to the new discoveries, they can be reduced to about fifty, or about one per cent. of the whole New Testament vocabulary—in itself a strong argument against the isolation in which "New Testament" Greek was formerly placed.

But this is very far from exhausting the significance of our new documents. In these, especially when taken along with the ostraca and inscriptions, we have abundant evidence as to many late Greek usages in the New

Testament, which at first strike us as strange, and also as to the exact shades of meaning to be attached to words, which have hitherto been understood imperfectly. To illustrate these and similar points in detail would, however, be hardly possible without a larger use of Greek than this book presupposes. And it will be better to confine ourselves to a few general examples, which show how fresh life and reality are imparted to some of our best-known New Testament words and phrases by tracing their usage in the ordinary Greek of the day. If I may repeat what I have said elsewhere : " We know our very familiarity with Scriptural language is apt to blind us to its full significance. But when we find words and phrases, which we have hitherto associated only with a religious meaning, in common, everyday use, and employed in circumstances where their meaning can raise no question, we make a fresh start with them, and get a clearer insight into their deeper application." [7]

Examples.—(1) Take, for instance, the common designation of Christians as " brethren " or " brothers " (ἀδελφοί). The practice no doubt was taken over from Judaism (Acts ii. 29, 37, *al.*) and from the example of our Lord Himself (cf. Matt. xii. 48, xxiii. 8); but we can at least see how the adoption of such a term was rendered easier by its application to the members of a funeral society, whose duty it was to take part in the embalming of dead bodies, or again to the " fellows " of a religious corporation in the Serapeum of Memphis.[8]

(2) So with the title " presbyter " (πρεσ-βύτερος). Without entering on the question of the presbyter's place and authority in the early Christian Church, it is obvious that the use of the word in civil life to denote a local or village officer must have prepared the way in Gentile circles for its acceptance in its new connotation. Thus in the year 117 B.C. a tax-farmer petitions the village-scribe and " the elders of the cultivators," that he may be assured of official " protection." Or, again, in 114 A.D. a woman lodges a complaint of assault and robbery against another woman whose husband as " elder " was responsible for the peace and order of the village. Or once more, in a document of 159-160 A.D.,

mention is made of the priests of the Socnopaeus temple as being divided into five tribes under the rule of five " elder-priests "—clearly a title not of age but of dignity. It is in this same document, we may note in passing, that the charge is laid against a fellow-priest " of letting his hair grow too long and of wearing woollen garments "—the former item recalling the fact that in the Early Church short hair was considered the mark of a Christian teacher, as compared with the unshorn locks of the heathen philosopher.[9]

(3) Keeping still to words with an ecclesiastical ring about them, the term " liturgy " has an interesting history. In classical times it was used of public services rendered gratuitously to the State, but later it came to be applied to all kinds of work or service, including those of a religious character, such as the " liturgy " of the Twin Sisters Thaues and Thaus, who held some position as attendants in the temple of Serapis at Memphis, with a corresponding right to certain allowances of oil and bread, which were apparently

frequently in arrears.[10] Similarly the corresponding verb is used in a contract of the year 8-9 A.D. with an *artiste* who undertakes to give her " services " (λειτουργεῖν) on certain specified occasions, including the festivals of the goddesses Isis and Hera, at a salary of forty drachmae a year, along with a further wage or present (ὀψώνιον) of thirteen drachmae two obols.[11]

Other more general uses of the word occur in connexion with the maintenance of the banks of the Nile, or with the release of persons from some public service " because it is not at present their turn to serve (διὰ τὸ μὴ ἐκπεσ[εῖ]ν αὐτοῖς τὸ νῦν λειτουργῆσαι)."[12] Very interesting too is a doctor's claim for exemption, on the ground that he was a doctor by profession, and had " treated medically " (ἐθεράπευσα: cf. Acts xxviii. 9 and Ramsay, *Luke*, p. 16 f.) the very persons who were now attempting to lay this new " liturgy " upon him (οἵτινές με εἰς λειτο[υ]ρ[γ]ίαν δεδώκασι).[13]

I admit, of course, that none of these instances adds materially to our knowledge of the word's connotation, but they give it fresh point, and enable us to understand how well-adapted it was to describe the "liturgy" or "ministry" of Christian fellowship (cf. 2 Cor. ix. 12, Phil. ii. 17, 30), and all the more so, because the word has now come to be almost wholly limited to a particular form of public worship.

(4) Its occurrence in the current phraseology of the time adds again a fresh reality to the Greek word (ἀρραβών), which is usually translated "earnest" in our English Versions. We have all been taught that by the "earnest" of the Spirit in such passages as 2 Cor. i. 22, v. 5, Eph. i. 14, we are to understand a part given in advance of what will be bestowed fully afterwards. But how increasingly clear this becomes when a woman who is selling a cow receives a thousand drachmae as an "earnest" (ἀραβῶνα) on the total purchase-money, or as when certain dancing-girls at a village entertainment receive so many drachmae "by way of earnest" (ὑπὲρ ἀραβῶνος) on their promised salary.[14]

(5) Another word, which has received new and vivid meaning, is the verb (ἀπέχω), which

in the Authorized Version of Matt. vi. 16 is rendered simply they " have " their reward, and in the Revised Version, a little more strongly, they " have received " their reward. But when we notice that the word was at the time the regular technical term for granting a receipt, as witnessed by innumerable papyri and ostraca, we can, with Deissmann, read into the passage in the Sermon on the Mount " the more pungent ironical meaning, *they can sign the receipt of their reward* : their right to receive their reward is realised, precisely as if they had already given a receipt for it " (*Bible Studies*, p. 229). Similarly, to refer to other instances of the same verb, in Phil. iv. 18 St. Paul expresses his gratitude to his beloved Philippians for their generous help in the words : " I give you a receipt in full for all things, and abound " ($ἀπέχω\ δὲ\ πάντα\ καὶ\ περισσεύω$) ; and in Philemon 15, the Apostle reminds Philemon that if Onesimus was parted from him for a time, it was only that he might " possess him "—as one for whom he had signed a receipt—for ever ($ἵνα\ αἰώνιον\ αὐτὸν\ ἀπέχῃς$).

(6) Another monetary phrase in the Epistle to Philemon is also worth noting when in v. 18 Paul bids Philemon, if Onesimus has done him any injury or is owing him anything— "set it down to my account" (τοῦτο μοι ἐλλόγα), where a verb is used closely allied to the verb which two women employ in a kindly letter bidding their steward "put down to our account" (ἡμεῖν ἐνλόγησον ἐπὶ λόγου), anything he has expended on the cultivation of the holding.[15] The metaphorical usage in Rom. v. 13, "but sin is not imputed (οὐκ ἐλλογεῖται) when there is no law" is also interestingly paralleled by a rescript of the Emperor Hadrian in which, after authorizing the announcement of certain privileges to his soldiers, he adds: "not, however, that I may appear to be making a reckoning against them (οὐχ ἕνεκα τοῦ δοκεῖν με αὐτοῖς ἐνλογεῖν)."[16]

(7) Much help can also be derived from the legal documents, which are so common amongst the papyri. Thus in his pioneer *Bible Studies* (p. 104 ff.), Deissmann has shown that the Greek adjective (βέβαιος) usually translated "sure" or "steadfast" in our English

"Common" Greek and New Testament

Versions, along with its cognate verb (βεβαιόω) and substantive (βεβαίωσις), is the regular technical term in the papyri to denote legally guaranteed security. Two examples will make this clear.

In an application for a lease belonging to the year 78 A.D., and therefore practically contemporary with the New Testament writings, provision is made for the publication of the lease for the legal period of ten days " in order that if no one makes a higher bid (ἐπίθεμα), the lease may remain guaranteed (βεβαία) to us for the period of five years without change,"[17] and, similarly, in a somewhat later document (266 A.D.), connected with the registration of a deed, it is laid down, " I will further guarantee the property always against all claims with every guarantee " (ἔτι τε καὶ παρέξομαί σοι βέβαια διὰ παντὸς ἀπὸ πάντων πάσῃ βεβαιώσει).[18] Read, then, the verb with this technical sense in view, and what added assurance it gives to the promise of 1 Cor. i. 7 f.: " Thus you lack no spiritual endowment during these days of waiting till our Lord Jesus Christ is revealed ; and to the very end he will guarantee (βεβαιώσει) that you are vindicated on the day of our Lord Jesus Christ" (Moffatt), just as another legal term (ὑπόστασις), which was used to denote the collection of papers bearing upon the possession of a piece of property, or as we would now say, the title-deeds, imparts a new certainty to the familiar definition—"Faith is the title-deeds (ὑπόστασις) of things hoped for" (Heb. xi. 1).[19]

(8) Considerable difficulty has been caused as to the exact meaning of Rom. xv. 28 when, with reference to the collection he had gathered among the Gentile Churches for the poor saints at Jerusalem, St. Paul writes to the Romans: "When I have sealed to them this fruit (σφραγισάμενος αὐτοῖς τὸν κάρπον τοῦτον), I will go on by you into Spain." Sanday and Headlam, following the usual meaning of sealing as an official mark of ownership (2 Cor. i. 22, Eph. i. 13), understand the Apostle to imply "that by taking the contributions to Jerusalem, and presenting them to the Church, he puts the mark on them (as a steward would do), showing that they are the fruit to the Church of Jerusalem of those spiritual

blessings (πνευματικά) which through him had gone forth to the Gentile world" (*Romans*, p. 413). But there is a specialized use of the verb in the papyri, as Deissmann (*Bible Studies*, p. 238 f.) has pointed out, which suggests another and more precise meaning. In a Fayûm papyrus, for example, of the second century A.D., Chairemon writes to Apollonios, " seal (σφράγεισον) the wheat and barley,"[20] which Deissmann explains : " seal (the sacks containing) the wheat and the barley," with a view to guaranteeing the correctness of their contents. And this conjecture can now be confirmed by a letter from Oxyrhynchus, in which a woman instructs a relative or friend : " if you come, take out six artabae of vegetable-seed, sealing it in the sacks (ἰς τοὺς σάκκους σφραγίσας) in order that they may be ready (πρόχιροι)."[21] The sealing was the proof that everything was in order, ready for delivery. Similarly St. Paul, " like a conscientious merchant," had seen to it that the gift entrusted to his care had been properly secured for those to whom it was assigned.

(9) In what are probably the earliest of his letters that have come down to us, the two Epistles to the Thessalonians, St. Paul finds it necessary to rebuke his converts for walking " in a disorderly manner " (2 Thess. iii. 11). The word (ἀτάκτως), with its cognates, is confined to these Epistles in the New Testament, and what exactly is meant by it is by no means clear at first sight. Is St. Paul referring to actual sin or moral disorder, or to something less heinous ? The papyri have supplied the answer in a striking manner. Among them is a contract of 66 A.D. in which a father arranges to apprentice his son with a weaver for one year. All the conditions of the contract are carefully laid down. The boy is to be supported and clothed during the whole time by his father, on condition that his master gives him five drachmae monthly on account of his keep, and twelve drachmae on account of his clothing at the expiry of the whole period. Then follows the passage which specially interests us. If there are any days during this period on which the boy " fails to attend " or " plays truant " (ὅσας δ'ἐὰν ἐν τούτῳ ἀτακτήσῃ

ἡμέρας), the father has to produce him for an equivalent number of days after the period is over. And the verb which is used to denote playing truant is the same verb which St. Paul uses in connexion with the Thessalonians.[22]

This then was their fault. They were idling, playing truant. The *Parousia* of the Lord seemed to them to be so close at hand that it was unnecessary for them to interest themselves in anything else. Why go to their daily work in the morning, when before night Christ might have come, forgetting that the best way to prepare for that coming was to show themselves active and diligent in the discharge of their daily work and duty.

(10) The reference to the *Parousia* may suggest another example. *Parousia*, as applied to the Return of the Lord, is simply the Anglicizing of a Greek word (παρουσία) which literally means "presence." But in late Greek the word had come to be applied in a quasi-technical sense to the "visit" of a king or great man. Thus in a papyrus of the third century B.C. we read of a district that was mulcted to provide a "crown" for one of

the Ptolemaic kings on the occasion of his "visit"; and in a letter of about the same date a certain Apenneus writes that he has made preparations for the "visit" of a magistrate Chrysippus (ἐπὶ τὴν παρουσίαν τοῦ Χρυσίππον) by laying in a number of birds for his consumption, including geese and young pigeons.[23]

It would seem, therefore, that as distinguished from other words associated with Christ's Coming, such as His "manifestation" (ἐπιφάνεια) of the Divine power and His "revelation" (ἀποκάλυψις) of the Divine plan, the "parousia" leads us rather to think of His "royal visit" to His people, whether we think of the First Coming at the Incarnation, or of the Final Coming as Judge.

(11) These examples are sufficient to show that it is often from the most unlikely quarters that light is shed upon our New Testament vocabulary, but it may be well to add yet other two remarkable and, indeed, somewhat extreme instances of this, to show that there are none of these papyrus scraps which may not have something to teach us.

There is, perhaps, no papyrus letter better known than the impudent letter of the schoolboy Theon to his father. We are not concerned with its contents as a whole at present; but there are two phrases in the letter which may well arrest us. The first is where the boy admits that, in view of his conduct, his mother had said to a friend, " He upsets me " (ἀναστατοῖ με), where the verb recalls the description of the Apostles as the men who had " upset " (ἀναστατώσαντες) the world—turned it upside down—by their preaching (Acts xvii. 6), and which St. Paul applies in the same metaphorical sense to the false teachers who are " upsetting " his Galatian converts (Gal. v. 12, οἱ ἀναστατοῦντες ὑμᾶς). The word is not a literary word, as you will find by consulting any Greek Lexicon, but it was a word in popular use, as the papyri show, and as such it adds a vivid touch to the New Testament passages.

But this is not all. Theon's mother goes on: " Off with him! " (ἆρρον αὐτόν)—the same expression—with such a whole world of difference in the application—as was used by the Jews with reference to Jesus, when they shouted: "Off with Him! Off with Him! Crucify Him!" (John xix. 5, ἆρον, ἆρον, σταύρωσον αὐτόν: cf. Acts xxi. 36, xxii. 22).[24]

(12) A boy has been living "riotously" (ἀσωτευόμενος: cf. Luke xv. 13). He has squandered all his own property, and is proceeding to squander the property of his parents. Accordingly, lest he "should deal despitefully" (ἐ[π]ηρεάσηι: cf. Luke vi. 28) with them, they find it necessary to issue a public notice that they will no longer be responsible for their son's debts, and they finish off by asking the local governor to have the notice "placarded up" where all may read it. The verb (προγραφῆναι) is a very expressive one, and is used by St. Paul in Gal. iii. 1: "Before whose eyes Jesus Christ was placarded up as crucified."

But while this meaning, as Bishop Lightfoot has shown (*Commentary ad loc.*), is well established in the general usage of the time, is there no gain to be able to add this new example to the Bishop's citations, occurring as it does in the very document which was to be placarded up, and which the kindly sands of Egypt have preserved for our instruction for some seventeen hundred years ?[25]

Grammar.—I have said nothing of the help which the papyri afford for the study of the grammar, as distinguished from the vocabulary, of the New Testament writers; but those who desire to understand the significance of our new documents in this connexion have only to consult the brilliant pages of Dr. Moulton's *Prolegomena*, or Dr. Robertson's *Grammar of the Greek New Testament in the Light of Historical Research* to see that here, again, the gains are of a very real character. The spelling and form of words, the construction of tenses and cases, the laxer use of prepositions, and many other points, can all be fully illustrated, and can all be cited as showing that we are dealing with the Greek language at an advanced period in its history, when many of the niceties of the Classical period were tending to disappear.

Literary Character of the New Testament.—This, however, is very far from saying that the later Greek which we associate with the papyri has

no rules of its own, or that, in the hands of the
New Testament writers, it is not often applied
with marked literary grace and power. The
writers, of course, differ largely in this connexion, in keeping with their individual
education and culture. At one end of the
scale, we have the rude Greek of St. Mark's
Gospel : at the other, the polished periods of
the author of the Epistle to the Hebrews. But
even in the case of the least literary writings
of the New Testament we must beware of so
emphasizing their popular character as to lose
sight of the grace and beauty imparted to them
in virtue of the subject-matter with which
they deal and the spiritual genius of their
authors. " In the Gospels," as Professor
Wellhausen has pointed out, " spoken Greek,
and even Greek as spoken amongst the lower
classes, has made its entry into literature." [26]
And another German scholar, Professor Jülicher, has borne similar testimony with
reference to the Pauline Epistles. " These
Epistles," he writes, " in spite of the fact that
they are always intended as writings of the
moment addressed to a narrow circle of

readers, yet approach much more nearly to the position of independent literary works than the average letters of great men in modern times. . . . Without knowing or intending it, Paul became by his letters the creator of a Christian literature." And more than that, Paul, as the same authority admits, " must be ranked as a great master of language, . . . and it is because his innermost self breathes through every word that most of his Epistles bear so unique a charm." [27] It is utterly unnecessary to labour the point. Such passages as the triumphant Hymn of Hope in Rom. viii. and the glorious Hymn of Love in 1 Cor. xiii. are moved by a heart-felt eloquence which makes them, regarded as literature, as notable as anything ever penned. And if we are told that the Pauline letters " differ from the messages of the homely Papyrus leaves from Egypt not as letters, but only as the letters of *Paul*," [28] we can accept the statement (though hardly in the sense the writer intended it), because it is just " Paul," and what Paul stands for, that does make all the difference.

The Surroundings of the New Testament Writers

The Ordinary Men and Women of the Time.— We have seen with the aid of the papyri that the New Testament as a whole is written in common Greek as it was spoken by the ordinary men and women of the time. But now what about these ordinary men and women themselves? Have the papyri any light to throw upon them? Hitherto they have been to us little more than a name. The historians of the period were concerned almost wholly with the leading men of the time, the great rulers, the great soldiers, the great writers, and they had neither space nor inclination to tell us how the common people lived. And yet it was to the common people that the Gospel was first preached (Mark xii. 37), and from amongst them that the Early Church gathered its most devoted adherents.

We must be careful not to exaggerate. There is clear evidence that not a few of those whom we are accustomed to describe as the Upper Classes were attracted by the preaching of the first missionaries, and enrolled themselves in the ranks of Christ's followers.[1] But that was not the general rule. And then, as so often since in the history of the Church, " not many wise after the flesh, not many mighty, not many noble-born " were called, but " God chose the foolish things of the world, that He might put to shame them that are wise ; and God chose the weak things of the world, that He might put to shame the things that are strong " (1 Cor. i. 26 f.).

But if so, anything that can help us to understand better the lives and the feelings of those people before the Gospel came to them is surely of the utmost importance. And it is just here again that the papyri aid us in the most unexpected ways. The great mass of them, as we have already seen repeatedly, are documents and letters of the most ordinary kind, written by the people, to the people, and about the people. And consequently they carry us right into the midst of the very class for whom our New Testament writings meant so much, and re-create for us the atmosphere in which these writings took their rise.

The Graeco-Roman World.—What then do we learn from the papyri in this connexion? One thing is clear. We must beware of drawing too uniform a picture of the world of the time. It had its lights and its shadows, its virtues and its vices, just like every other period in the history of mankind.

There is only too abundant evidence to support the statements of the Roman satirists, for example, regarding the wickedness, the unblushing wickedness, of the times, and the gloom and misery with which it was accompanied.

> On that hard Pagan world disgust
> And secret loathing fell.
> Deep weariness and sated lust
> Made human life a hell.

But while this is so, we must not forget that

this applies principally to the " Roman noble," to the state of morals in high places, and that, at the other end of the social scale, there was the large, hitherto unnoticed, class of humble men and women, whom those wonderful papyrus scraps have restored to us in the flesh. In looking at them, as they stand thus revealed, we are brought face to face with what we may call average humanity, with its daily duties and its daily trials, its hopes and its fears, its affections and its quarrels—just, indeed, what we find in the homely illustrations of the Gospel parables.

The Census Papers.—Actual examples of this will meet us directly, but before we pass to them, reference may be made, in connexion with the population as a whole, to the census papers, which suggest points of peculiar interest for the New Testament student.

These census papers cover a period of two and a half centuries, and it has now been established beyond a doubt that during the reign of Augustus house-to-house enrolments were made at regular intervals of fourteen years in Egypt, and, therefore, in all probability in Syria also. The earliest return which as yet has come to light is dated in the year 20 A.D., but there is independent evidence that there was a census in 6 A.D. (cf. Acts v. 37), and there is also very general agreement that there was yet an earlier, taken, in accordance with the general cycle of fourteen years, in 8 B.C. If so, this would be the enrolment to which St. Luke refers in the beginning of the second chapter of his Gospel, and would point to that year as the real date of the Birth of Christ.

A difficulty, however, at once arises. According to the Lucan account, the census was taken when Quirinius was Governor of Syria, and non-Christian historical evidence has hitherto pointed to his occupying that office in 6 A.D., the date of the second, not the first census. In his monograph *Was Christ born at Bethlehem?* (2nd Edit., London, 1898), Sir William M. Ramsay tried to meet the difficulty on the ground that at the earlier date Quirinius held a military command in Syria, which might be brought within the meaning of the word translated " was governor " (ἡγεμονεύοντος) in Luke ii. 2. But we are now relieved of the need of any such expedient, as the same authority has pointed out, for recently inscriptions have come to light showing that Quirinius acted as governor of Syria-Cilicia and Galatia for the first time between 10 B.C. and 7 B.C., and in all probability in 9-8 B.C., the enrolment year. Therefore, although there are still difficulties, we may take it that the general evidence of the papyri is confirmed, and that our Lord was born some eight years before the date suggested by our ordinary chronology.[2]

One further corroboration of the Lucan narrative from our new sources may be noted. The statement that " all went to enrol themselves every one to his city " (Ch. ii. 3) has often been regarded as indicating that Herod carried out the enrolment on national lines as a concession to Jewish sentiment ; but if we may judge from a notice in a Roman official's letter-book of 104 A.D., it would appear that Herod, when he issued his order, was in reality acting in accordance with Roman practice.

The rescript, which is, unfortunately, much mutilated, runs as follows :—

> Gaius Vibius Maximus, Prefect of Egypt (says) : Seeing that the time has come for the house to house census, it is necessary to compel all those who for any cause whatsoever are residing out of their districts to return to their own homes, that they may both carry out the regular order of the census, and may also attend diligently to the cultivation of their allotments.[3]

Into other questions raised by the census papers we cannot enter at present, but, as showing the general form which they followed, a specimen may be of interest. It belongs to the census of 48 A.D.

> To Dorion strategus and . . . royal scribe and Didymus and . . . topogrammateis and komogrammateis from Thermoutharion the daughter of Thoonis with her guardian Apollonius the son of Sotades. There are living in the house which belongs to me in the South Lane . . .
>
> Thermoutharion, a freedwoman of the above-mentioned Sotades, about 65 years of age, of medium height, dark-complexioned, long-visaged, a scar on the right knee. Total—three persons.
>
> I the above-mentioned Thermoutharion along with my guardian the said Apollonius swear by Tiberius Claudius Caesar Augustus Germanicus Emperor that assuredly the preceding

document makes a sound and true return of those living with me, and that there is no one else living with me, neither a stranger, nor an Alexandrian citizen, nor a freedman, nor a Roman citizen, nor an Egyptian, in addition to the aforesaid. If I am swearing truly, may it be well with me, but if falsely, the reverse.

In the ninth year of Tiberius Claudius Caesar Augustus Germanicus Emperor, Phaophi. . . .[4]

Family Life. Husbands and Wives.—Passing to the general family life of the time, almost every phase of it meets us in some form or another in our documents. Thus our earliest dated Greek papyrus is a marriage contract in which strict provisions are laid down to regulate the life of the married pair—provisions, it is worth noticing, which tend to be weakened or to disappear in the growing laxity of the Roman period, only to be revived again under Christian influence. As showing the manner in which the woman's position was safe-guarded, " equal legal rights " were accorded in the contract before us to both husband and wife in the preservation of the contract and in the bringing of charges against each other.[5]

That unfortunately recourse was had to this

privilege in many cases is proved by the numerous "writings of divorcement" (cf. Matt. v. 31), in which the spouses renounce all claim upon each other—the cause being occasionally ascribed to the intervention of " some evil demon " (ἐκ τινὸς πονηροῦ δαίμονος), by whom the " good hopes " of what had been expected to be a life-long union had been wrecked.[6]

Even where matters had not gone so far, the curtain is lifted upon many a matrimonial dispute, long supposed to have been for ever buried with those who took part in it ; as when a deserted wife complains that her husband has so prolonged a period of " retreat," presumably for religious purposes, in the Serapeum at Memphis, as to bring her and her children to the last extremity, notwithstanding all her own efforts for their support ;[7] or as when a similar complaint is addressed by a husband to his wife, who had been away from home for a month, and whose return he eagerly desires. " I assure you," he writes, " that ever since you left me I have been in mourning, weeping by night and lamenting by day." And then, as practical proof of his grief, he adds, " Since we bathed together on July 12th I neither bathed nor anointed myself (οὐκ ἐλουσάμην οὐκ ἤλιμε (*l.* ἤλειμμαι) until Aug. 12th."[8] Or may it be that all this is mere parade, and that this husband is like the hypocrites whom our Lord condemns, not because they fast, but because they fast ostentatiously ? They " disfigure " (ἀφανίζουσιν) their faces by neither anointing nor washing [that they may " figure " (φανῶσιν) in the eyes of men (Matt. vi. 16).

To take a very different example, how clearly a wife's anxiety comes out in a letter, included among the Giessen papyri, which a certain Aline addresses to her husband Apollonius. I give it in Dr. H. I. Bell's translation.

> I am constantly sleepless, filled night and day with the one anxiety for your safety. Only my father's attentions kept my spirits up, and on New Year's Day I assure you I should have gone to bed fasting but that my father came in and compelled me to eat.   I implore you therefore to take care of yourself and not to face the danger without a guard ; but just as the strategus here leaves the bulk of the work to the magistrates, you do the same.

We are not told the exact nature of the danger

to which Apollonius was exposed, but it is probable that it was occasioned by his being on military duty in connexion with the revolt of the Jews during the reign of Hadrian. If so, the letter is an excellent example of the manner in which our documents introduce us to important historical events in the most casual way, and let us see them not from the point of view of the professed historian, but as they affect an otherwise unknown and obscure individual. Aline " may probably enough," as Dr. Bell remarks, " have shared the popular detestation of what one of these letter-writers calls the ' impious Jews,' but her prime concern is not for the fortunes of their rising, still less for the issues involved in the struggle between the majesty of the Roman power and the chosen people ; she is not even anxious that Apollonius should, in the cant phrase of the war, ' do his bit ' ; for to her he is not a character of history at all, but a concrete individual, her husband and the father of her children." [9]

Parents and Children.—When we pass to the relations between parents and children, we are at once arrested by a letter, dating from the very beginning of the Christian Era (1 B.C.), in which a man writing to his wife, who was expecting the birth of a child, proceeds : " If —good luck to you !—you bear offspring, if it is a male, let it live (ἄφες) ; if it is a female expose (ἔκβαλε) it." [10] Rebukes directed against this, as a common heathen practice, are to be found in early Christian writers, but, so far as the papyri are concerned, this seems to be almost a solitary instance of it. Indeed, in a previous part of this very letter, as showing the light in which children were generally regarded, the writer enjoins : " I beg and beseech of you (ἐρωτῶ σε καὶ παρακαλῶ σε: cf. 1 Thess. iv. 1), " Take care of the little child, and as soon as we receive wages (ὀψώνιον λάβωμεν : cf. 2 Cor. xi. 8) I will send them to you " ; and similarly in a third century letter, written in the most illiterate Greek, a man, after enjoining his sister to see that his slave-girl (πεδείσκην, *l.* παιδίσκην) was properly industrious, adds : " If Tamaoun bear a child, make her be assiduous (φειλοπονῆσε, *l.* φιλοπονῆσαι) with it." [11]

What, too, from the children's side could be more dutiful than the letter addressed by a son to his father, an architect by trade, who had carefully filed it amongst his correspondence?

> I am glad if you are in good health and everything is to your mind. We ourselves are in good health. . . . Write to us yourself that we may know how you are and not be anxious. Take care of yourself that you may be in good health, and come to us strong.[12]

Still warmer is the tone of a letter recently acquired by the British Museum, in which the writer reproves his brothers for their thoughtless treatment of their mother, for "we ought to reverence our mother like a goddess, especially such a good mother as ours."[13] And the same considerate desire to allay unnecessary maternal anxiety leads a soldier-boy in the early years of the second century A.D. to write "to his lady mother" (τῆι μητρὶ καὶ κυρίᾳ: cf. 2 John 1) reassuring her regarding his health, of which, much to his annoyance, she had received bad accounts. "I blame the person who told you," he continues, "Do not trouble (μὴ ὀχλοῦ) to send me anything." And then, to make the matter quite certain, he repeats the injunction in a postscript in an even stronger form, " Do not burden yourself (μὴ ἐπιβαροῦ) to send me anything." [14]

It must not be thought, however, that the papyri do not also show other, and less pleasing, sides of human nature, as in another soldier's letter to his mother, which for persistent and unblushing begging would be hard to beat. After the customary greetings, the lad demands two hundred drachmae along with a military cloak and certain other articles. Various reproaches as to previous treatment are then uttered, and in particular he is very bitter regarding his father's treatment of him on the occasion of a recent visit to the camp. " When my father came to me, he did not give me an obolus or a cloak or any thing. All will laugh at me. His father is a soldier (στρατεύεται : cf. Luke iii. 14) they will say, and yet he gives him nothing. My father said, When I get home, I will send you everything, but he has sent me nothing. Why ? The mother of Valerius sent him a pair of girdles, and a jar of oil, and a basket of dainties, and two hundred drachmae. Wherefore I beg you, mother, send to me. Do not leave me thus," and so on, ever in the same whining strain.[15]

Apart altogether, from its tone the letter in the original Greek—and may I again emphasize that it is with the actual letters themselves as they left their first writers' hands that we are dealing—leaves much to be desired in the way of spelling and grammar, and shows that the parents' zeal for the proper education of their children, to which other papyri bear evidence, was not always successful.

Education.—"Take care not to offend any of the persons at home," writes Cornelius to his sweetest son Hierax, "and give your undivided attention to your books, devoting yourself to learning, and you will have profit from them." And the advice is made the more palatable by the announcement of the dispatch of clothes and money.[16]

In another letter a mother writes to her son, whose teacher (καθηγητής) had just left him.

> I took care to send and ask about your health and learn what you are reading; he said that it was the sixth book (of Homer) and testified at length regarding your pedagogue (περὶ τοῦ παιδαγωγοῦ σου). So my son, I urge both you and your pedagogue to take care that you go to a suitable teacher. Many salutations are sent to you by your sisters and Theonis' children, whom the evil eye shall not harm (ἀβάσκαντα: cf. Gal. iii. 1 τίς ὑμᾶς ἐβάσκανεν;), and by all our friends by name (*i.e.* individually, κατ' ὄνομα: cf. 3 John 15). Salute your esteemed pedagogue Eros. . . . [17]

The reference to the pedagogue is specially interesting, as showing that it was his duty not merely to take the boy to school, but to act towards him as a general tutor or guardian, until he shall have reached maturity, in the same sense in which in the familiar Galatian passage Ch. i. 24 St. Paul represents the law acting as a " pedagogue " to bring men to their full growth and freedom in Christ.

Slaves.—But the papyrus has a further significance. The pedagogue would be a slave and the manner in which he is referred to, and the esteem in which he is held, may well remind us that the lot at least of the superior class of slaves was by no means so hard as it is sometimes represented—and was often accompanied by the kindliest dispositions on both sides. Few letters show more genuine feeling than the letter addressed by a female slave to her sick master: it belongs to the second century, probably to the time of Hadrian.

> Tays to the lord Apollonius, many greetings. Above all I greet you master, and am praying always for your health. I was distressed, lord, in no small measure, to hear that you were sick; but thanks be to all the gods that they are keeping you from all harm. I beseech you, lord, if you think it right, to send to us, if not, we die, because we do not see you daily (cf. 1 Cor. xv. 31). Would that we could fly and come and pay our reverence to you. For we are distressed. . . . Wherefore be reconciled to us, and send to us. Good-bye, lord. . . . All is going well with us. Epeiph 24.[18]

With this may be compared a letter addressed by a patron to a woman called Aplonarion who, the editors think, may have been his emancipated slave. The letter, they add, is "the most sentimental that has yet appeared among published papyri." We can only find room for a few sentences.

> I rejoiced greatly at receiving your letter. . . . But I was very much grieved that you did not

come for my boy's birthday, both you and your husband, for you would have been able to have many days' enjoyment with him. But you doubtless had better things to do ; that was why you neglected us. I wish you to be happy always, as I wish it for myself, but yet I am grieved that you are away from me. If you are not unhappy away from me, I rejoice for your happiness, but still I am vexed at not seeing you.[19]

The whole process of the manumission of slaves as illustrating the new freedom which comes to Christ's bondmen forms one of the most interesting and striking sections in Deissmann's *Light from the Ancient East* (pp. 324-334), but as it is based principally on the evidence of inscriptions at Delphi, it lies beyond our immediate province.[20] Mention may, however, be made in passing of the additional light thrown by papyri on two important and difficult New Testament passages.

The first is the phrase generally rendered " first fruits of the Spirit " (ἀπαρχὴ τοῦ πνεύματος) in Rom. viii. 23, in connexion with which Professor Stuart Jones has shown, on the evidence of a section in the Code of Regulations dealing with the Department of Special

Revenues in Roman Egypt, that the word here translated "first fruits" (ἀπαρχή) is the technical term for the birth-certificate of a free person. Accordingly, he interprets the general meaning of the passage in Romans as follows :—

"When we read the passage which begins at verse 16, we see that St. Paul is here arguing that our claim to spiritual freedom is based on the witness of the Spirit to our spirit, just as in Egypt the testimony (μαρτυροποίησις) of the parent was among the documents put in evidence in the procedure of examination (ἐπίκρισις) by which claims to privileged status were judged ; and that in spite of this —in spite of the fact that we have, as it were, obtained through the mediation of the Spirit the certificate which entitles us to be registered as the Sons of God—we are still awaiting our formal release from the bondage of the flesh and the law."[21]

Our second passage is the familiar verse, Gal. vi. 17, where, according to the rendering of the Revised Version, St. Paul exclaims : "From henceforth let no man trouble me (κόπους μοι μηδεὶς παρεχέτω) : for I bear (βαστάζω) branded on my body the marks (τα στίγματα) of the Lord Jesus." It is often thought that the reference is to the practice of branding slaves with a letter or mark to show to whom they belonged. But Deissmann (*Bible Studies*, p. 352 ff.) prefers to appeal to a third century papyrus in the Leiden Museum, in which the words occur: " I bear (βαστάζω) the corpse of Osiris . . . should so-and-so trouble me (κόπους παράσχῃ), I shall use it against him." As, that is, the carrying of a particular amulet associated with the god acts as a charm against the trouble caused by an adversary, so St. Paul finds himself protected against similar attacks, because he carries on his body the marks of Jesus. [22]

Social Life.—In passing to the social life of the period, we are at once met by the numerous dinner and marriage invitations. Here is one of the former class, where the entertainment seems to have been of a ceremonial rather than of a private nature.

> Antonius, son of Ptolemaeus, invites you to dine with him at the table of the lord Serapis

in the house of Claudius Serapion on the 16th at 9 o'clock (= 3 p.m.).[23]

Almost every word in that short note has something to tell us. The Greek verb (ἐρωτᾷ) with which it opens is used in its late sense of "invite," "request," as in the New Testament (Luke xi. 37, 1 Thess. iv. 1, 12, *al*.). "The table of the lord Serapis" carries us back to "the table of the Lord and of demons" in 1 Cor. x. 21, though the actual word for "table" (κλίνη) is different. The designation "lord" (κύριος) applied to Serapis is one proof out of many of the widespread use of the word as a divine title at the beginning of the Christian Era, leading to St. Paul's protest (1 Cor. viii. 5 f.) against the "gods many, and lords many" (θεοὶ πολλοὶ καὶ κύριοι πολλοί) with which Christianity found itself confronted in contrast to the "one Lord, Jesus Christ" (εἷς Κύριος Ἰησοῦς Χριστός), whose "name is above every name" (Phil. ii. 9).[24] And the elliptical phrase "in the (house) of Claudius Serapion (ἐν τοῖς Κλαυδίου Σαραπίωνος) confirms the rendering of the Revised Version in Luke ii. 49, "Wist ye not that I must be in My Father's house (ἐν τοῖς τοῦ πατρός μου)?"

Taxation.—It is tempting to go on to the marriage and birthday feasts, and to the village festivals with their pantomimes, musicians and dancing girls ; but the other, the darker, side of the picture demands our attention. Thus, to mention one feature which is constantly recurring in our new sources, the papyri are full of references to the heavy taxation which was imposed upon the Egyptians during the Roman period—names of more than 150 different taxes are now known—and also to the oppressive way in which it was often levied. A Paris papyrus, for example, of the second century B.C., throws a vivid light on the practices of tax-gatherers, as, after special mention of those who petition at the custom houses (πρὸς ταῖς τελωνίαις : cf. Matt. ix. 9), instructions are given that no one should be wronged (ἀδικῆται) by the tax-gatherers attempting " to lay a false accusation " (συκοφαντεῖν).[25] That this is the real meaning of the last word, and not as often thought " to exact wrongly," is confirmed by other documents, and shows that the rendering of the Authorized Version is to be preferred to the Revised in Luke iii. 14, xix. 8.

As proving further how readily corruption arose among Government officials, reference may be made to a Tebtunis papyrus of the second century A.D., in which a priest connected with temple finance is warned of the approaching visit of a government inspector, but told not to be anxious, as he can count upon the writer's good offices with the inspector. In Grenfell and Hunt's translation it runs:

> You must know that an inspector of finance in the temples has arrived and intends to go to your division also. Do not be disturbed on this account, as I will get you off. So if you have time write up your books and come to me; for he is a very stern fellow. If anything detains you, send them on to me and I will see you through, as he has become my friend. If you are in any difficulty about expense and at present have no funds write to me, and I will get you off now as I did at first. I am making haste to write to you in order that you may not put in an appearance yourself; for I will make him let you through before he comes to you. He has instructions to send recalcitrants under guard to the high-priest.[26]

Comment is surely unnecessary. How clearly the situation stands out before us ! What a picture of laxity and corruption in the official world !

Petitions.—In view of these things is it to be wondered at that there are constant petitions for redress, and that the " protection " of the governing powers is eagerly sought ? A special instance, which brings us into close touch with one of our Lord's parables, will illustrate this.

The lot of the widow has always been peculiarly hard in the East, and in a Rylands papyrus of the third century A.D., we find a certain Aurelia appealing to the Prefect for protection against the aggression of Syrion, a magistrate of the village in which she lives. According to her story, her husband had acted as shepherd for Syrion, but when he " went the way of men," Syrion seized sixty sheep and goats which belonged to the deceased, and not content with this wished, " by means of his local influence," to lay hold of her and her children's property while her husband was still lying unburied. All her appeals for restitution had ended in failure, and no other course had been open to her than to petition the Prefect for assistance. The appeal was so far successful that in an endorsement added to the document in a different hand of writing the Prefect gives instructions that the matter should be investigated, with the result, as we learn from another papyrus, that an order for legal restitution was made. So far, however, from acquiescing, the defendant Syrion interposed new obstacles and further proceedings had to be instituted. Have we no commentary here on the "importunate widow" of the Gospel story? Do we not hear again, this time in actual life, her repeated cry, "Do me justice of mine adversary!" (Luke xviii. 3) ?[27]

Many similar illustrations might easily be brought forward, but another aspect of our documents demands attention, and that is the manner in which they show us the men and women of the day face to face with such ever-present problems, as the sense of bereavement and the sense of sin.

Sense of Bereavement.—In the first instance, a certain Taonnophris and her husband Philo have apparently lost a son, and a friend Irene, who had herself suffered bereavement, writes to condole with them in the following terms.

> Irene to Taonnophris and Philo, good cheer! I was as much grieved and wept over the blessed one, as I wept for Didymas, and everything that was fitting I did and all who were with me, Epaphroditus and Thermouthion and Philion and Apollonius and Plantas. But truly there is nothing any one can do in the face of such things. Do you therefore comfort one another. Farewell. Hathyr 1 (=October 28).
>
> (Addressed) To Taonnophris and Philo.[28]

Very touching is it not? The desire to mourn with those who mourn, and yet the feeling of utter helplessness in the presence of what death brings—" Truly there is nothing any one can do in the face of such things." How unlike the calm tone of assurance with which St. Paul comforts the Thessalonian mourners in like circumstances: " We would not have you ignorant, brethren, concerning them that fall asleep; that ye sorrow not even as the rest "—Irene, Taonnophris, Philo, and all similarly situated—" which have no hope. For if we believe that Jesus died and rose again, even so them also that are fallen asleep in Jesus will God bring with him " (1 Thess. iv. 13, 14).

Sense of Sin—A second letter strikes an even deeper note. A son writes to his mother to tell her of the sad plight into which he has fallen, due, he frankly admits, to his own fault. He is ashamed to come home, but will not his mother forgive him? The last part of the letter has been much destroyed, and only a few words of the concluding lines have survived, but, as you read, you will have little difficulty, I think, in filling up the gaps for yourselves:

> Antoni(u)s Longus to Nilous his mother, many greetings. Continually I pray for your health. Supplication on your behalf I direct each day to the lord Serapis. I wish you to know (γεινώσκειν σαι θέλω: cf. Phil. i. 12) that I had no hope that you would come up to the metropolis. On this account neither did I enter into the city. But I was ashamed to come to Karanis, because I am going about in rags. I write you that I am naked. I beseech you, mother, be reconciled to me (διαλάγητί μοι: cf. Matt. v. 24). But I know what I have brought upon myself. Punished I have been every way. I know that I have sinned (οἶδα ὅτι ἡμάρτηκα: cf. Luke xv.

18, 21). I heard from Postumus who met you in the Arsinoite district, and unseasonably related all to you. Do you not know that I would rather be a cripple than be conscious that I am still owing any one an obolus ? ... Come yourself ... I have heard that ... I beseech you ... I almost ... I beseech you ... I will ... not ... otherwise. ...

 (Addressed) To ... his mother from Antonius Longus her son.[29]

I know, of course, that doubts have been cast on the boy's good faith, and that he has been represented as practically a fraud, trying to win favour for selfish ends. But I confess that I cannot read the letter that way. It seems to ring true. And if so, what a self-revealing document it is ! How inevitably it suggests comparison with our Lord's own story of the Prodigal Son—the poor wanderer forgiven and welcomed home !

Questions in Temples.—In view then of these things, is it wonderful that there should have been in the period with which we are dealing a widespread perplexity and restlessness, leading people to have recourse to dreams and oracles and questions addressed to the local deities ? One striking example of the last-named practice has been the actual discovery within the ruins of the temple of Bacchias of a question, written in very illiterate Greek, which a suppliant had deposited there in the first century A.D.

> To Sokanobkoneus the great great god. Answer me (χρημάτισόν μοι: cf. Matt. ii. 11, 22), Shall I remain in Bacchias? Shall I meet (him)? Answer me this.[30]

And from the same source comes this further question of a slightly later date:

> O lords Dioscuri, is it fated for him to depart to the city? Bring this to pass, and let him come to an agreement with thy brother.[31]

Magical Papyri.—But more significant still are the magical papyri, which have been recovered in such numbers. In themselves the contents of these papyri are often puerile to a degree, but as a testimony to the anxieties of the human heart, turning in all directions for help, they are invested with a deep pathos. A few lines from the great Paris magical papyrus of the third century will show their character.

> A notable spell for driving out demons. Invocation to be uttered over the head (of the possessed one). Place before him branches of

olive, and standing behind him say: Hail, spirit of Abraham; hail, spirit of Isaac; hail, spirit of Jacob; Jesus the Christ, the holy one, the spirit . . . drive forth the devil from this man, until this unclean demon of Satan shall flee before thee. I adjure thee, O demon, whoever thou art, by the god Sabarbarbathiôth. . . . Come over, O demon, for I shall chain thee with adamantine chains not to be loosed, and I shall give you over to black chaos in utter destruction.[32]

The strange admixture of pagan, Jewish, and even Christian elements in this spell will be observed by all, while the whole class of literature to which it belongs shows how applicable to the men and women of the day is the epithet ($\delta\epsilon\iota\sigma\iota\delta\alpha\iota\mu\text{ον}\acute{\epsilon}\sigma\tau\epsilon\rho\text{οι}$) which St. Paul uses of the Athenians in Acts xvii. 22, and which no single English term can adequately render—" too superstitious " and yet " exceedingly god-fearing," and so prepared for the fuller revelation of the one God Who can alone meet their deepest needs.[33]

These, let me again repeat, are only specimens of the way in which the papyri help us in reconstructing the environment of our New Testament books. They may seem, perhaps, of little moment as compared with the outstanding character of the books' contents. But they have in reality a closer bearing upon the interpretation of these contents than may at first sight appear, and in any case everything that bears upon the historical setting of writings which mean so much for us cannot fail to awaken our interest and command our attention. The " treasure " may be " in earthen vessels," but that only proves the more convincingly that " the exceeding greatness of the power " is " of God and not from ourselves " (2 Cor. iv. 7).

Christian Documents on Papyrus

Christianity in Egypt.—We have tried to see what we can learn from the papyri regarding the form, the language, and the surroundings of our New Testament writings. And, apart from all other gains, the very effort to look at these writings in connexion with the times which produced them, and from the standpoint of those to whom they were first addressed, can hardly have failed to deepen in our minds the sense that we are dealing with real, living, historical documents.

But there is still another way in which the new discoveries may help us. Among the papyri which have been brought to light are a certain number of Christian origin, which are of the utmost importance in tracing the history of Early Christianity in Egypt. Their witness was much required. Beyond the tradition that St. Mark was the first to proclaim the Gospel in that country, and the practical certainty that the new teaching found its first and principal supporters among the Jewish communities which were so numerous in the Nile valley, we have hitherto had to content ourselves with a few scattered references to apocryphal and heretical writings for our information regarding the progress of Christianity in Alexandria and Egypt up till almost the close of the second century.[1] And though in comparison with the hundreds of classical texts and the tens of thousands of non-literary documents which are now in our hands, these Christian remains seem at first sight singularly few and unimportant, that is a state of things which fresh discoveries may rectify any day, while what we have acquired is at least sufficient to dispel our ignorance in various directions, and to bring home to us, with a definiteness and vividness impossible before, the independent growth of a Church, which in not a few particulars stood outside the ecclesiastical conditions prevailing throughout the Empire.

This would, of course, be clearer if appeal were made to all the new evidence now available, to documents on parchment or vellum, to inscriptions, and to the Coptic ostraca, as well as to the Greek papyri; but it is to these last that we must confine ourselves strictly at present.[2]

New Testament Texts.—In turning to Christian documents on papyrus, we naturally begin with those which have preserved for us some portion of the New Testament text. Of these between thirty and forty have now been deciphered and edited, though, unfortunately with one exception, to which reference will be made directly, they are of a very fragmentary character.[3] Notwithstanding this, six at least are of outstanding interest, if only because they belong to the third century, and are, therefore, from a hundred to a hundred and fifty years older than the great vellum manuscripts, such as the Codex Vaticanus or the Codex Sinaiticus, on which we are mainly dependent for our knowledge of the New Testament in the original Greek.

Amongst the new documents is the leaf of

a papyrus book which, at the time of its discovery, was reckoned " to be a fragment of the oldest known manuscript of any part of the New Testament," and from which there still start up clearly before our eyes the words with which the New Testament opens : " The book of the generation of Jesus Christ, the son of David, the son of Abraham " (ΒΙΒΛΟC ΓΕΝΕCΕWC ΙΥ͞ Χ͞Υ Υ͞Υ ΔΑΥΙΔ [ΥΙΟΥ] ΑΒΡΑΑΜ).[4]

Still more significant, as preserving the original roll form of the New Testament books, are the scanty remains of two consecutive columns from a roll containing the Gospel of St. John, of which we show a reproduction in the frontispiece to this volume.[5] The remains of the first column contain parts of Chap. xv. 25-xvi. 2, and in the second line the reader will have little difficulty in making out the words ΟΤΑΝ ΕΛΘΗ Ο Π[ΑΡΑΚΛΗΤΟΣ, "when the Comforter is come." The second column extends from v. 21 to v. 31 of Chap. xvi., a passage which is also covered in another third century fragment recently published, written, so Professor Hunt informs me, in a somewhat similar hand. This last papyrus has the further interest of being the earliest copy of a Gospel, which, to judge from the number of fragments recovered, must have quickly gained a leading place in the affection of the Early Church.[6]

It meets us again in the sheet of a papyrus book with John i. 23-31, 33-41, on the left-hand leaf, and John xx. 11-17, 19-25, on the right-hand leaf, which Dr. Grenfell and Dr. Hunt again assign to the third century, though Professor Gregory inclines to a somewhat later date.[7]

From the manner in which the sheet has been folded the editors conclude that the Codex, when complete, consisted of a quire of twenty-five sheets, the first of which was left blank or contained only the title. Thus we have not only an interesting testimony to the early method of book-production, but, if the calculation be correct, the quire must have originally contained, as Deissmann has pointed out, Chap. xxi., and so forms an additional, and the earliest, witness to the fact that the Fourth Gospel was never, so far as we know, circulated without this closing chapter, which forms an epilogue or appendix to it.[8]

From the end of the third or the beginning of the fourth century comes a part of Heb. i. 1, written in a small uncial hand on the margin of a letter written from Rome (cf. p. 145 f.). If we were sure that the quotation was added to the letter in Rome, the point might be of interest in connexion with the Roman destination of the Epistle, which has found many supporters.[9]

And very little later is the largest find made as yet in New Testament texts, about one-third of the Epistle to the Hebrews, copied out on the back of a roll, the *recto* of which contains the new Epitome of Livy. The text agrees closely with the Codex Vaticanus in the portions common to both, while it fortunately supplements it in the later chapters, from Ch. ix. 14 to the end, which are wanting in that Codex.[10]

A curious feature of the papyrus is the manner in which the text is broken up by means of double dots into a number of divisions ($\sigma\tau\iota\chi o\iota$), which frequently coincide with the rhythmical divisions which Blass, with perhaps greater excuse than in the case of the Pauline Epistles, claims to have discovered in Hebrews.[11]

It is impossible to go over all these early fragments in detail, but three belonging to the fourth and subsequent centuries may be mentioned. The first is a papyrus containing Rom. I. 1-7 (except part of verse 6) written out in large rude letters, which suggest to the editors that it may have formed a schoolboy's exercise. Deissmann, on the other hand, prefers to see in it an amulet or charm, belonging to a certain Aurelius Paulus, who is named in a different hand of writing in a note below the text (cf. p. 39 ff.). In either case, the document is a striking example of the strange sources from which our new light on the New Testament comes—a school exercise or an amulet! In addition to the evidence of the writing, the date can in this case be fixed with great precision from the fact that the papyrus was found tied up with a contract dated in 316 A.D.[12]

The second document consists of the remains of two leaves of a papyrus book of

St. John, belonging probably to the sixth century, whose small size recalls the desire, of which we have evidence elsewhere, to possess copies of the new writings in a portable form. The two leaves are not consecutive, the first containing John iii. 14-17^a with verses 17^b-18 on the *verso*, and the second containing Ch. iii. 31-32; but fragmentary though they thus are, it is surely something to be able to re-read one of the most familiar Gospel passages, " God so loved the world, that He gave His only-begotten Son," from the very document which conveyed that triumphant assurance to some early Egyptian believer.[13]

Similarly with our third example, a papyrus from the Rainer Collection at Vienna, dating from the sixth century, in which the stories of the Pharisee and the Sinful Woman (Luke vii. 36-44) and of Mary and Martha (Luke x. 38-42) are arranged in such a way as to suggest that we have here an example—perhaps the earliest in existence—of an *Evangelistarium* or Gospel reading-book, arranged for liturgical purposes. The text is in closest agreement with the text as we now read it.[14]

Looking back at these texts we may sum up their importance from four points of view.

1. The probability is that they are for the most part fragments of New Testaments intended for private, rather than for Church use. They may, therefore, be described as poor men's Bibles, and show us the form in which the Scriptures were generally circulated before the advent of the great official codices of the fourth century.

2. If *textually* they present us with no new readings of special interest they supply confirmation from a very early date of our critical text, and at the same time lend a certain amount of support to the view so widely held that the principal authorities for that text, such as the Vatican and Sinaitic Codices, are of Egyptian origin. Their relation further to these two manuscripts, agreeing now with the one independently and now with the other, and occasionally differing from both, may be taken as a much-needed warning not to pin our faith too exclusively to any one manuscript or group of manuscripts.

3. Apart from their witness to the text our fragments are of interest *palæographically* as showing what Dr. Grenfell and Dr. Hunt have called " the prototype " of the handwriting of the great vellum codices. " Though no doubt the literary hand, as practised upon vellum, reacted upon the papyrus script, we should say," they tell us, " that the debt of papyrus to vellum was unappreciable as compared with that of vellum to papyrus."[15]

4. They prove to us that so far from the codex or book-form coinciding in point of time with the general use of parchment for literary purposes, it was, so far at least as theological works are concerned, in widespread use from a very early date.[16] All the fragments of which we have been speaking, with the exception of the third century St. John fragment and the fourth century text of Hebrews, both of which formed parts of rolls, were written in leaves of papyrus codices, and, with other early documents, such as the so-called Sayings of Jesus, point to this being the favourite form for the early circulation of

Christian writings, both canonical and non-canonical.

Non-canonical Texts.—Of Non-canonical Texts, that is texts of writings which form no part of our received New Testament, we have again considerable traces, though it must be admitted great dubiety still exists as to the exact place and value to be assigned to the varied writings, of which they form part.

One of the most interesting of these fragments belongs to the Rainer Collection in Vienna, and was published by Dr. G. Bickell, Professor of Christian Archaeology in the University of Innsbruck, as far back as 1885.[17] Though now only a few broken lines remain, they are sufficient to show that the papyrus contains a narrative somewhat similar to Mark xiv. 26-30, which, according to Bickell's amended reading, may be translated as follows :—

> Now after eating according to custom (μετὰ δὲ τὸ φαγεῖν, ὡς ἐξ ἔθους): You will all be offended (σκανδαλισθήσεσθε) this night, as it is written, I shall smite the shepherd, and the sheep shall be scattered. Peter said, Though all (are

offended), yet not I. He (the Lord) said to him, The cock shall cry twice, and thou shalt be the first to deny me thrice.

The similarities to, and yet differences from, the Synoptic accounts are apparent. There is no mention, for example, of the promise of Jesus to go before His disciples into Galilee, which is inserted both by St. Matthew (xxvi. 32) and St. Mark (xiv. 28) after the Old Testament quotation, and the words used regarding the cock's crowing are different (πρὶν or πρὶν ἢ δὶς (Mark) ἀλέκτορα φωνῆσαι in the Gospels: ὁ ἀλεκτρυών δὶς κοκκύξει in the Fragment). And the question is at once raised, What is the relation of the Fragment to the Gospels? Is it derived from them? Or does it represent an earlier tradition, which lies behind the Gospels, and may even have played a part in their production? Professor Bickell himself emphatically advocates the latter view. The concise and energetic nature of the account is pointed to as favouring its great antiquity. And the Fragment is best explained, he thinks, as a third century copy of a document emanating originally from the first century, and belonging to the same class of narratives (διηγήσεις) which St. Luke describes in his Preface (Ch. i. 1, 2) as lying behind the Third Gospel.

So eager, indeed, is Dr. Bickell to find a place and a name for his discovery, that he makes the startling suggestion that in it we may actually have part of a Greek translation of the Aramaic *Logia* of St. Matthew, to which Papias refers in a well-known passage. And though Harnack does not go the length of accepting this suggestion in its entirety, he too concedes a pre-canonical date to the Fragment, and regards it as an instance of the kind of rough material out of which our Gospels were afterwards constructed.[18]

But, weighty though Harnack's opinion on such a point undoubtedly is, it cannot be said that this view has met with anything like general acceptance. The very features of the document which have been taken as proving its priority to our Synoptic accounts have also been urged in support of a date subsequent to them. And Dr. Hort will carry many with him in the belief that we have here the remains of some Early Christian writing in which the words of St. Peter and of his Master are quoted in a free and condensed form.[19]

The fact is that the evidence is far too scanty to enable us to form any decided opinion the one way or the other. And we must wait in the hope that future discoveries may throw fresh light on what is undoubtedly a very interesting relic of ancient Christian Egypt.

From about the same period, that is not later than 250 A.D., although the original composition was much earlier, we have eight fragments of a papyrus roll, containing a lost Gospel, very similar in point of form to the Synoptic narratives, but ascribing to our Lord at least one striking saying not found in them. Jesus has been addressing his disciples in a speech which concludes with teaching closely parallel to certain sentences in the Sermon on the Mount. The disciples thereupon ask, " When wilt Thou be manifest to us, and when shall we see Thee (πότε ἡμῖν ἐμφανὴς ἔσει καὶ πότε σε ὀψόμεθα;) " ? And, in answer to this question, Jesus is described as saying,

"When ye shall be stripped and not be ashamed . . . (ὅταν ἐκδύσησθε καὶ μὴ αἰσχυνθῆτε. . .)."

The end of the sentence unfortunately is lost, but what remains is enough to show that we have a Saying which, if not derived from a very similar passage in the Gospel according to the Egyptians, or from the collection of Sayings used by the author of Second Clement, is so closely related to what we find in these two authorities as to suggest an original source from which all have borrowed. If so, the saying may well have distinct elements of genuineness in it, and in any case this three-fold testimony makes it, as its discoverers have pointed out, one of the most important and best attested of the early *Agrapha*, or Sayings ascribed to Christ, which are not found in the Canonical Gospels.[20]

To a closely similar, if not the same, source may be ascribed certain fourth century fragments of a papyrus book, in which, amongst other novelties, reference is made to a vision of Jesus to one who was cast down—" And Jesus stood by in a vision and said, Why art thou cast down (τί ἀθ[υμ]εῖς;)? For it is not thou who ... but he who gave (?) ..." The gaps make it impossible to determine who was intended, or what were the circumstances under which the vision was granted. But there is a certain plausibility in the view urged by Dr. Bartlet that we have here an otherwise unrecorded appearance of the Risen Lord granted to St. Peter, by which he was restored from the remorse of his denial. The further suggestion that the fragments may belong to the Apocryphal Gospel of St. Peter, a large portion of which was discovered at Akhmîm in Upper Egypt in 1886, seems to the editors on various grounds, both external and internal, very doubtful, and it is safer to acquiesce meanwhile in their conclusion of *non liquet*.[21]

Sayings of Jesus.—But significant though these discoveries are, none of them has awakened anything like the same general interest as the two Oxyrhynchus fragments, containing what purport to be Sayings of Jesus.

The first of them was brought to light in 1897 (cf. p. 14), and with exemplary promptitude was published by the discoverers, Dr. Grenfell and Dr. Hunt, in the same year with an illuminating Introduction and Commentary.[22] And six years later the same editors were able to publish a second fragment of a very similar character discovered in almost the same place, and belonging apparently to about the same date, which is assigned on palæographical grounds to the period between 150 A.D. and 300 A.D., probably soon after 200 A.D.[23]

The contents of the two Fragments cannot be quoted here. It must be enough to state that they contain a number of Sayings directly ascribed to Jesus, each Saying being prefaced by the words " Jesus saith," while the second series has a general introduction to the effect: " These are the (wonderful ?) words which Jesus the living (Lord) spake to ... and Thomas, and He said unto (them), Every one that hearkens to these words shall never taste of death."

In themselves the Sayings present the same general features which have already met us in the fragments of the Non-canonical Gospels, certain of the Sayings being very closely related to the Synoptic tradition, while others are wholly new, and distinguished in certain particulars by an ascetic or encratite tendency.

Into the many questions that have arisen regarding their interpretation it is, of course, impossible to enter here, nor can I attempt to discuss at length the various theories that have been put forward regarding their character and source.[24] But, speaking generally, the choice may be said to lie between seeing in them extracts from some early Gospel, and regarding them as part of a collection of Sayings of Jesus, as such, put together at a very early date for some practical purpose.

So far, at least as regards the first collection, the former view, the view of extracts, was strongly advocated by Harnack, who derived them from the Gospel of the Egyptians,[25] while Zahn preferred to think of the Ebionite Gospel[26] and Dr. Taylor of the Gospel of St. Thomas, a view which obtains a certain amount of support from the introduction to the Second Series.[27]

If, however, we are to look for an analogy to the general character of the Sayings it is to be found in the similar collections of Sayings made by Jewish Rabbis, such as the *Pirke Aboth* or *Sayings of the Fathers*, rather than in narrative Gospels.[28] And, on the whole, the general probabilities of the case point strongly in the direction maintained in the *Editio Princeps*, that we have here parts of a Collection or Collections of Sayings of our Lord, which may originally have numbered several thousands, and, while differing in many respects from the known Gospels, contained nothing to connect them with any particular sect or party in the Church.[29]

If this be so, when we keep in view the generally simple and archaic character of the Sayings, combined with their early date, it is hardly possible not to find in them again at least a residuum of genuineness. And even though they cannot be said to add substantially to our knowledge of the teaching of Jesus, they at least show the channels by means of which that teaching was popularly diffused at a very early period, and in the hands of more than one expositor have proved themselves still capable of profitable homiletic application.[80]

Theological Works.—As regards new fragments of early theological works, I must be content with merely mentioning certain passages largely made up of Biblical quotations, which may go back to the latter part of the second century, and, if so, form the oldest Christian writing hitherto published—a third century leaf of a papyrus book embodying teaching closely resembling that regarding a tree being known by its fruits in Matt. vii. 17-19 and Luke vi. 43-44—another leaf belonging to the end of the same century or the beginning of the following century, in which the words occur, " For the spirit of prophecy is the essence of the prophetic order, which is the body of the flesh of Jesus Christ, which was mingled with human nature through Mary," suggesting that we have to do here with a Christian Homily on the spirit of prophecy, perhaps, as Harnack suggests, Melito's lost treatise " Concerning Prophecy " (περὶ προφητείας)—a fragment of much the same date, which deals with the " upper " and " lower " soul in a way to suggest Gnostic influence—and another example of heretical Gospel literature in the form of a tattered papyrus leaf, " copied probably in the early decades of the fourth century," in which, in answer to the disciples' question, " Lord, how then can we find faith ? " the Saviour replies, " If ye pass from the things that are hidden and into the light of things that are seen, the effluence (ἀπόρροια) of conception (ἔννοιας) will of itself show you how faith . . . must be found . . . He who has ears to hear, let him hear. The lord of all is not the Father but the Fore-father (προπάτωρ); for the Father is the beginning of what shall be . . ."[31]

Liturgical Works.—Works of a liturgical character cannot be said to bulk largely in our new sources. But amongst the Rainer papyri is a leaf containing two antiphons, one of which apparently was sung by the choir in connexion with the observance of the Feast of Epiphany. It runs as follows :—

> O Thou, who wast born in Bethlehem, and brought up in Nazareth, and who dwelt in Galilee, we have seen a sign from heaven. When

the star appeared the shepherds keeping watch over their flocks wondered. Without kneeling they said: Glory to the Father, Hallelujah! Glory to the Son and to the Holy Spirit, Hallelujah! Hallelujah! Hallelujah!

The text has been assigned palæographically to the third century, and a pre-Arian and pre-Athanasian date has also been claimed for it on the ground that after this period the Catholic party would not have inserted the Alleluia between the name of the Father and that of the Son and the Holy Ghost, nor would the Arian party have assigned equal glory to the Divine Persons of the Godhead. Dr. Bickell, indeed, regards the fragment as an Antiphon Song in connexion with the Psalms, which intervened between the reading of the Old and New Testament lessons, and was intended to enforce some Christian lesson to which these Psalms pointed. If this be a correct view it is of importance as carrying back the liturgical system of the Church to an earlier date than is sometimes supposed, for if such a practice were in full use in the third century it had probably already a considerable history behind it.[32]

Hymns.—From the fourth century comes an elaborate metrical acrostic arranged according to the letters of the alphabet, embodying various Gospel precepts and ending with a contrast between the final lot of the wicked and the saints.[33]

The general character of the Hymn has led Harnack to conjecture that we have here a Baptismal Hymn, or more particularly an Exhortation to Candidates for Baptism, somewhat on the lines of the teaching contained in the earlier chapters of the *Didache* (chaps. i.-v.), but marked by a more definite Christology as in the striking lines—

> God came bringing many blessings, He wrought a triple victory over death. . . .
> Jesus who suffered for this, saying, I give my back, that thou fall not a prey to death.[34]

This has been generally regarded as, outside the Lucan Hymns, the oldest Greek Christian Hymn known, but recently there has been published a Christian Hymn, belonging to the latter part of the third century, which has the additional interest of being accompanied by musical notation. It is thus " by far the most ancient piece of Church music extant, and may be placed among the earliest written relics of Christianity." Unfortunately, like so many of the other documents we have been considering, it is only a fragment, but enough remains to show that the powers of Creation are called upon to invoke Father, Son, and Holy Ghost and that the usual ascription of power and praise is assigned " to the only giver of all good " (δωτῆρι μόνῳ πάντων ἀγαθῶν).[35]

Prayers.—Various old Christian prayers have also come to light, amongst which may be mentioned the third century fragment of what appears to have been a collection of liturgical prayers for use in church, one of which is headed " Prayer of the Apostles, Peter, and the rest."[36] And though there is nothing in the contents to suggest this Apostolic origin the Prayer undoubtedly goes back to a very early date, as shown, for example, in the numerous citations from the Old Testament and the reminiscences of New Testament diction.

This same use of Biblical language also distinguishes a short prayer found at Oxyrhynchus, which is assigned by the editors to the end of the third or the beginning of the fourth century. It runs in their translation :—

> O God Almighty, who madest heaven and earth and sea and all that is therein, help me, have mercy upon me, wash away my sins, save me in this world and in the world to come, through our Lord and Saviour Jesus Christ, through whom is the glory and the power for ever and ever. Amen.[37]

And with this may be compared another short prayer, also from Oxyrhynchus, of about a century later, in which God is pointedly invoked as the sender of the trials from which the petitioner seeks deliverance :—

> O God of the crosses that are laid upon us help thy servant Apphouas. Amen.[38]

According to the editor the prayer is inscribed " in large rude uncials," and the same feature marks yet a third Oxyrhynchus prayer, written in illiterate Greek on the *verso* of a papyrus sheet, which had apparently been originally used for keeping accounts or some similar purpose.

> O Lord my God and my hope, look on Thecla and her children, look on Anna and her servant,

look on Apphous, look on Sakaon, look on Dionysius and his children, look on Helladius, look on Ptolemæus, look on each one of them.[39]

Of a more formal character are the remains of two prayers discovered on the leaf of a papyrus book at Hermopolis, and belonging to the end of the fourth century. From the manner in which the two prayers are divided up into small sections by dots to guide the reader the prayers were evidently intended for public use in church. And from the fact that the second prayer is definitely headed σαββατικὴ εὐχή, "A Prayer for Saturday," and that the distinct mention of fasts in the earlier prayer readily associates it with Friday's fast, the editor has suggested that we may have here the remains of a collection of prayers, designed for use on the different days of the week, which may go back originally, if not to the second, then at latest to the third century.[40]

Creeds.—We may add here a sixth century copy of the Nicene Creed, which shows considerable independence, not coinciding throughout with any other version, and is followed by a personal statement to the effect :—

> This is my creed, with this language [I shall approach without fear (?)] the terrible judgment-seat of the Lord Christ in that dread day when He shall come again in His own glory to judge the quick and the dead and to reign with the saints for ever and ever. Amen.[41]

And still older, going back to the second half of the fifth century, are six lines of a copy of the so-called Constantinopolitan Creed, which was first affirmed in 381 A.D., and afterwards passed into currency both in East and West as the authorized version of the Nicene Faith.[42]

Church Organization.—The help hitherto derivable from the papyri regarding the general organization of the Church cannot be said to amount to much, but mention may be made of a fourth century letter, showing the presbyters of the Church (τ[ο]ὺ[ς] πρεσβυτέρους τῆς ἐκκλησίας) acting as the guardians of public morals (cf. p. 65 f.) in certain very extraordinary circumstances connected with the misconduct of the two daughters of a certain Sarapion.[43]

And with this may be compared a homily, addressed apparently to ascetics in the fifth or sixth century, warning them against the wiles of the female sex. A few lines will show its character.

> By a woman he [the Evil One] turned aside the most wise Solomon (?) to transgression ; by a woman he shaved and blinded the most brave Samson ; by a woman he dashed to the ground and (slew) the sons of Eli the priest. . . . A wicked woman is the worst of all (ills ?), the . . . of all ; and if she also have wealth as her ally in wickedness, the evil is double. . . .[44]

Of a wholly different character is an interesting fifth or sixth century inventory of property belonging to the village church of Ibion, and entrusted to the care of " the most reverent John, presbyter and steward." Amongst the articles scheduled in it are twenty-one parchment books ($\beta\iota\beta\lambda\iota\alpha\ \delta\epsilon\rho\mu\alpha\tau\iota(\nu\alpha)\ \overline{\kappa\alpha}$), as against three on papyrus ($\chi\alpha\rho\tau\iota\alpha\ \overline{\gamma}$), showing the increasing use of parchment for religious purposes by this date (cf. p. 54).[45]

But of far greater importance is an official calendar of Christian Assemblies or Services ($\sigma\upsilon\nu\alpha\xi\epsilon\iota\varsigma$), which were held at Oxyrhynchus in 535-6 A.D. in connexion with the visit of the Alexandrian Patriarch Timotheus IV.

It requires a liturgical expert to appreciate the full value of the light thus thrown on the various church festivals mentioned, but the mere number of churches with which these are associated in this one Egyptian tour is in itself a striking proof of the rapid progress of Christianity. If during a period of about five months 66 assemblies, on about 62 different days, were distributed among at least 26 different churches, then in a year, as the editors point out, the whole number of assemblies may have exceeded 130, and of churches 40.[46]

Many other documents might be quoted to illustrate the influence Christianity was exerting, as, for example, the new and stringent provisions regulating married life which appear in marriage contracts (cf. p. 89), or the modifications in the lot of slaves, as when, in a deed of manumission of 354 A.D., we find the formula " free under earth and heaven according to the service due to God the compassionate."[47]

But let me pass on rather to another set of documents, which, perhaps, more than any others have brought us face to face with the actual lives of individual men and women in the early Christian communities. I mean the *libelli*, or certificates of having sacrificed in the heathen manner in order to escape molestation during the Decian persecution in 250 A.D.

Libelli.—The use of such *libelli* was well known, if only from the account in Cyprian's letters (*Epp.* 30(3), 55(2)). And now the literary evidence has been confirmed in the most striking manner by the recovery of a number of the *libelli* themselves.

Their official character is shown by the general sameness of form and phraseology, while the fact that they are all dated between 13th and 15th June, 250 A.D., proves that all refer to the same set of circumstances.

As an example it is sufficient to quote the well-preserved specimen edited and translated by Dr. Hunt in the first volume of the Rylands Papyri.

> To the commissioners of sacrifices from Aurelia Demos, who has no father, daughter of Helene

and wife of Aurelius Irenæus, of the Quarter of the Helleneum. It has ever been my habit to sacrifice to the gods, and now also I have in your presence, in accordance with the command, made sacrifice and libation and tasted the offering, and I beg you to certify my statement. Farewell.

'(2nd hand). I, Aurelia Demos, have presented this declaration. I, Aurelius Irenæus, wrote for her, as she is illiterate.

'(3rd hand). I, Aurelius Sabinus, prytanis, saw you sacrificing.

'(1st hand). The first year of the Emperor Caesar Gaius Messius Quintus Trajanus Decius Pius Felix Augustus, Pauni 20.[48]

It may, of course, be urged that we have no definite proof that all those who availed themselves of these certificates were Christians; they might have included suspected pagans, and the comparatively large number (20) of *libelli* found in a single little village such as Theadelphia has been advanced as proof of a very extended use of them. But after all there was not likely to be much difficulty in the way of conforming to the decree on the part of the pagan population, and any such evidence on their part might well seem superfluous, whereas it was notoriously against the Christians that the edict was aimed. And the fact, of which so much has been made, that a certain Aurelia, priestess of Petesuchos, is named as a *libellatica*, though at first sight strange, is explicable on the ground that this Aurelia had been a convert from Paganism to Christianity, and in making her declaration of " orthodoxy " made use for greater security of her old title.[49]

In any case, whatever interpretation may be put on certain of these *libelli*, nothing can rob them of their importance as authoritative documents, in which, through their different signatures, all the persons concerned stand out clearly before us in connexion with a striking, if painful, incident in the history of the Christian Church.

Christian Letters.—The same human interest distinguishes in a marked degree the Christian letters that have come down to us. There is no form of writing so self-revealing as a true letter, written without any thought of a wider public than its original recipient, and with no other aim than to meet some immediate and occasional need. And though again the specimens of private Christian letters are very few in number as compared with those emanating from pagan sources, they introduce us to surroundings and circumstances of which otherwise we should have known practically nothing.

The oldest of these letters hitherto published is included in the Amherst Collection, and is addressed by an Egyptian Christian at Rome to his fellow-Christians in the Arsinoite nome between the years 264 (265) and 282 (281) A.D.[50] The text is unfortunately much mutilated, nor can it be said that the contents, so far as they can be deciphered, are in themselves of any special interest; they are mainly occupied with certain business transactions in corn and linen. But the letter at least shows us these early believers engaged in the ordinary avocations of life, " in the world " though not " of the world," and actually using as their intermediary in money matters no less a person than Papas Maximus, the Bishop of Alexandria. " This is certainly," says Deissmann, " not a bad indication of the way in which the scattered churches held together socially " (the letter, it will be remembered, was written from Rome to the Fayûm) " and of the willingness of the ecclesiastical leaders to help even in the worldly affairs of their co-religionists." [51]

To a special study by the same authority we owe the widespread interest taken in another letter of a slightly later date, in which Psenosiris, a Christian presbyter, writes to Apollo, a brother presbyter at Kysis, to tell him of the safe arrival of a certain woman in the Great Oasis. By converting a designation of bad character (πολιτική) into a proper name (Πολιτική), Deissmann concludes that we have to do here with a Christian woman who had been banished to the Great Oasis during the Diocletian Persecution, and who, for greater security, had been sent into the interior pending the arrival of her son. If this be a correct interpretation of the situation we are met by the striking fact that, at latest by the beginning of the fourth century, Christianity had penetrated into the Libyan Desert into " a most forlorn corner on the extremest southern border of the known world," where it was represented by, amongst others, "the good and faithful" of a gravediggers' Guild, while amongst its adherents was this humble woman, otherwise unknown, who, unlike the *libellatici*, had stood firm, and, in consequence, had suffered banishment. "It is a proof," as Deissmann characteristically remarks, "of Christianity's inexhaustible power of bending to the lowly and of ennobling what is commonplace."[52]

The same may be said of the fourth century letter of Demetrius to Flavianus, which is interesting not only on account of its numerous echoes of New Testament phraseology, but also as illustrating the new attitude Christianity had brought about between servant and master.

> To my lord Flavianus Demetrius sends greeting. As on many other occasions so now still more plainly the favour of the Lord God towards you has been revealed to all of us, in that my mistress has recovered from the illness that struck her down, and may it be granted to us evermore to continue acknowledging thanks to Him, because He was gracious to us, and paid heed to our prayer in preserving our mistress : for in her we all of us centre our hopes. But

pray, my lord, do you pardon me and receive me kindly, although unwillingly I cast you into such distress by writing regarding her the messages which you received. For my first messages I despatched when she was in great affliction, not being master of myself, and being anxious that by every means in your power you might succeed in coming to us, this being what duty demanded. But when she seemed to have taken a turn for the better, I was anxious that other letters should reach you by the hands of Euphrosynus, in order that I might make you more cheerful. For by your own safety, my lord, which chiefly concerns me, unless my son Athanasius had then been in a sickly state of body, I would have sent him to you along with Plutarchus, at the time when she was oppressed by the sickness. But now I am at a loss how to write more regarding her, for she seems, as I said before, to be in a more tolerable state, in that she has sat up, but nevertheless she is still in a somewhat sickly state of body. But we are comforting her by hourly expecting your arrival. That you may be in continued health, my lord, is my prayer to the Master ($δεσπότῃ$) of all.
Pharmouthi 6.

The letter is addressed on the back:

To Flavianus from Demetrius.[53]

Other letters of a similar character will be found in the later volumes of the Oxyrhynchus Papyri, and mention should also be made of the extensive correspondence of Abinnaeus, a Christian officer in the Assinoite district. From this last there has been recovered at least one gem, the touching letter, in which, after the manner of Paul to Philemon, Papa Caor, the village priest of Hermopolis, begs Abinnaeus to pardon " just this once " a military deserter who had taken refuge with him, and whom he is now sending back to his duties. Apart from the contents, the use in this letter of the title Papa ($\pi\acute{a}\pi as$) to describe a humble village priest, as compared with its " episcopal " connotation in the first Christian letter already cited, deserves to be noted.[54]

Still another side of Christian life in Egypt meets us in the traces which our documents exhibit of the extent to which early believers took over with them into their new faith old pagan practices and superstitions.

Questions in Churches.—Thus in counterpart to the heathen custom of consulting the local deity in times of difficulty by means of questions deposited in his shrine (cf. p. 109 f.), we find such a prayer as the following, which was presumably originally left in some Christian Church :—

> O God, the all ruling, the holy, the true One, merciful and creative, the Father of Our Lord and Saviour Jesus Christ, reveal to me Thy truth, whether Thou wishest me to go to Chiout, or whether I shall find Thee aiding me and gracious. So let it be. Amen.[55]

Amulets.—In the same way there is abundant evidence of the continued use of amulets or charms to be worn about the person for protection against sickness and other ills— the Lord's Prayer, or some other passage from the Gospels, frequently taking the place of the magical incantations in the old charms.

One of these amulets, belonging possibly to the fifth century, has been edited by Dr. Hunt in the *Oxyrhynchus Papyri*, viii. No. 1151. It consists of a narrow strip of papyrus about $10\frac{3}{8}$ inches long, and never more than 2 inches across, and, when found, was tightly folded and tied with a string. In Dr. Hunt's translation it runs as follows :—

> "Fly, hateful spirit ! Christ pursues thee ; the Son of God and the Holy Spirit have out-

stripped thee. O God of the sheep-pool, deliver from every evil thy handmaid Joannia whom Anastasia also called Euphemia bare. In the beginning was the Word, and the Word was with God, and the Word was God. All things were made by him and without him was not anything made that hath been made. O Lord Christ, Son and Word of the living God, who healedst every sickness and every infirmity, heal and regard thy handmaid Joannia whom Anastasia also called Euphemia bare, chase from her and put to flight all fevers, and every kind of chill, quotidian, tertian, and quartan, and every evil. Pray through the intercession of our lady the mother of God and the glorious archangels and Saint John, the glorious apostle and evangelist and divine, and Saint Serenus and Saint Philoxenus and Saint Victor and Saint Justus and all the Saints. Upon thy name, O Lord God, have I called, the wonderful and exceeding glorious name, the terror of thy foes. Amen." [56]

As showing the strange intermixture of magical, Jewish and Christian elements which survived even as late as the end of the fifth or the beginning of the sixth century, I may add the short incantation, which comes next in the same collection :—

" Oror phor, eloi, adonai, Iao sabaoth, Michael, Jesus Christ, help us and this house." [57]

Here I must bring this catalogue of texts—for I fear it has been little more—to a close. It has been impossible within the necessary limits to discuss their many and varied features of interest as one would have liked. But I hope that enough has been said to prove to the student of Early Christianity, if such proof were needed, what a rich and fruitful field of investigation lies ready to his hand in the new discoveries.

Here and There among the Papyri

Notes

NOTES ON CHAPTER I

1. See further Pliny *Naturalis Historia*, xiii. 11-13, and cf. F. G. Kenyon, *The Palaeography of Greek Papyri* (Oxford, 1899), p. 14 ff.

2. *Geneva Papyri*, i. No. 52^3 (iv./A.D.) χάρτιον καθαρὸν μὴ εὑρὼν πρὸς τὴν ὥραν, εἰς τοῦ [τ]ον ἔγραψα. The reading is amended by Wilcken, *Archiv für Papyrusforschung*, iii. p. 399.

3. *Oxyrhynchus Papyri*, i. No. 79 (181-192 A.D.): cf. Milligan, *Selections from the Greek Papyri* (Cambridge, 1910), No. 35.

4. *Oxyrhynchus Papyri*, ii. No. 326 (about 45 A.D.).

5. The Herculaneum papyri are mostly occupied with philosophical writings of the Epicurean school, notably with the works of Philodemus, whose library they may have formed. There are, moreover, a few fragments of Epicurus himself, including the letter to a child (see Milligan, *Selections*, No. 2), which in its artless simplicity may well be compared with Luther's well-known letter to his " dear little son."

6. It was published under the title *Charta papyracea Graece scripta Musei Borgiani Velitris*, ed. N. Schow, Romae, 1778.

7. *The Flinders Petrie Papyri*, i. (Dublin, 1891), p. 11.

8. The sonnet begins "Departing summer hath assumed," and will be found in the Oxford edition of Wordsworth's *Poems*, p. 498 f.

9. Egypt Exploration Fund: *Archaeological Report*, 1896-97, p. 6.

10. *Tebtunis Papyri*, i. p. vi. f.

11. Full particulars of the various papyrus publications will be found in the *Archiv für papyrusforschung* (Leipzig, Teubner, 1901-), edited by Professor U. Wilcken, and in the recently started Italian review *Aegyptus* (Milan, 1920-), where a very full Bibliography of current Papyrology is supplied. The principal collections with the customary abbreviations, and a list of some of the more important monographs on the subject are detailed in Milligan, *Selections*, p. xi. ff. See also the brief selected Bibliography in the present volume, p. ix. ff.

12. Reference should be made to the useful *New Chapters in the History of Greek Literature*, edited by J. U. Powell and E. A. Barber (Oxford, 1921). Mr. Powell also contributes a popular account to *Discovery*, iii. (1922), p. 8 ff., entitled, "New Light on the Silver Age of Hellas." See further Professor R. Y. Tyrrell, *Essays on Greek Literature* (London, Macmillan, 1909), pp. 85 ff., 134 ff.

13. More recently Sir F. G. Kenyon has published a paper on "Greek Papyri and their contribution to Classical Literature" in the *Journal of Hellenic Studies*, xxxix. (1919), p. 1 ff., and in the same number, p. 16 ff., there is an important article by Professor B. P. Grenfell on "The Value of Papyri for the Textual Criticism of Extant Greek Authors," where it is shown that the texts of the chief

authors have not undergone extensive changes since the second century, but that there is evidence for much less stability at an earlier period. The subject is also dealt with by W. Schubart, *Einführung in die Papyruskunde* (Berlin, Weidmann, 1918), p. 86 ff., and V. Martin, *Les manuscrits antiques des classiques grecs* (Geneva, Kundig, 1919).

14. Article on " Papyri and Papyrology," in *The Journal of Egyptian Archaeology*, i. (1914), p. 84.

15. Mr. Norman M'Lean informs me that the text of the fragments is on the whole conformable to that of the oldest uncials A and B, but that he and his colleague, Canon Brooke, have not yet arrived at a definite conclusion which of the two they are nearer to.

16. Of the 1828 papyri in *Oxyrhynchus Papyri*, i.-xv., it has been calculated that 224 are private letters—208 from the first four centuries and 16 from a later period. The Ptolemaic letters, which have been recovered to the number of 72, are edited by S. Witkowski in *Epistulae Privatae Graecae*, 2nd Edit. (Leipzig, Teubner, 1911).

NOTES ON CHAPTER II

1. *Handbook to the Textual Criticism of the New Testament*, 2nd Edit. (London, Macmillan, 1912), p. 33 ff.

2. The thoroughness of the State postal service is shown by an interesting register of about 255 B.C. published in *Hibeh Papyri*, i. No. 110. " Careful note is made of the day and hour of the arrival of each messenger, his name and that of the clerk who received and issued letters at the office, the number and addresses of the packets, and the

names of the messengers to whom they were handed on. The day-book in the registered letter department of a modern post office can hardly be more methodical and precise " (Edd.).

3. As, for example, in Deissmann's well-known discussion in *Bible Studies* (Edinburgh, 1901), p. 3 ff.

4. *The Letters to the Seven Churches of Asia* (London, 1904), p. 25 : cf. the same writer's *The Teaching of Paul in Terms of the Present Day* (London, 1913), p. 425 f.

An interesting example of the extension of a letter from the individual to the general is afforded by a letter addressed by George Fox to Lady Claypole, the favourite daughter of Oliver Cromwell, at a time when she was sick and troubled in mind. When it was read to her, she said, " it staid her mind for the present. Afterwards many Friends got copies of it, both in England and Ireland, and read it to people that were troubled in mind ; and it was made useful for the settling of the minds of several " (*The Journal of George Fox*, London, Headley Brothers, 1902, i. p. 434).

5. *Oxyrhynchus Papyri*, iv. No. 746 : see also Milligan, *St. Paul's Epistles to the Thessalonians* (Macmillan, 1908), p. 127. For other good examples of letters of commendation cf. *Oxyrhynchus Papyri*, ii. No. 292 (about 25 A.D.) (=Milligan, *Selections*, No. 14), and the Christian letter, *ib.* viii. No. 1162 (iv./A.D.).

6. *Berliner Griechische Urkunden*, i. No. 332 (=Milligan, *Thessalonians*, p. 128).

7. *Berliner Griechische Urkunden*, ii. No. 423 (ii./A.D.) (=Milligan, *Selections*, No. 36).

8. Reference may be made to Dean Armitage Robinson's Excursus "On some current epistolary phrases" in his edition of *St. Paul's Epistle to the Ephesians*, p. 275 ff.: cf. also J. Rendel Harris, "A Study in Letter-Writing" in *Expositor*, V. viii. p. 161 ff.

9. Cf. *Oxyrhynchus Papyri*, ii. No. 275$^{42f.}$ (66 A.D.), ἔγραψα ὑπὲρ αὐτοῦ μὴ ἰδότος γράμματα : *Berliner Griechische Urkunden*, i. No. 209$^{6f.}$ (158-9 A.D.), ἔγραψα ὑπὲρ αὐτοῦ ἀγραμμάτου. This use of ἀγράμματος = "unlettered" or "illiterate" would seem to indicate that it is to be understood in the same sense in Acts iv. 13, and not merely as "unacquainted with Rabbinic learning."

10. *Rylands Papyri*, ii. No. 183 (*a*).

11. I am tempted to quote from Professor M. D. Buell's beautiful and suggestive little book on *The Autographs of Saint Paul* (New York, Eaton and Mains, 1912), as I fear it is not generally accessible: "The salutation, 'Grace to you!' can be as fully established as true, distinctive, and personal a voucher of Paul's individuality as any peculiar and personal trait of his handwriting.... Paul's exclusive and recurrent use of the word 'CHARIS' ('Grace') as a formula of salutation and mark of personal identity is not unlike the terse sentiment which the Black Prince coupled with his signature in a document which he signed in A.D. 1370: '*De par homont ich dene*' ('With high honour do I serve'). What more appropriate salutation, as sounding the innermost deeps of his life in Christ, and concentrating into one phrase the ruling passion of Paul's apostolic ministry, could have been devised?" (pp. 15, 17).

12. See an article by the late Bishop Moule in *The Churchman* for June, 1906.

13. Cf. Milligan, *New Testament Documents*, p. 242 ff.

14. *Oxyrhynchus Papyri*, iv. No. 724.

15. A good example is afforded by the letter of the olive-planter Mystarion (*Berliner Griechische Urkunden*, i. No. 37, cf. p. 353), reproduced by Deissmann, *Light from the Ancient East*. "Mystarion's letter, with its greeting and the rest of the conclusion in a different writing, namely in Mystarion's own hand, was written only a few years before St. Paul's second letter to the Christians of Thessalonica, and it proves that somebody at that date closed a letter in his own hand without expressly saying so" (p. 158 f.).

16. *Studies in the Synoptic Problem*, by Members of the University of Oxford (Oxford, 1911), p. 3 ff.

17. The alternative endings, including the ending from the recently discovered Freer or Washington manuscript, are discussed in *New Testament Documents*, p. 274 ff.

18. See *Berliner Griechische Urkunden*, iv. Nos. 1206 and 1207, with the editor's notes on pp. 344 and 347. The date of the correspondence is 29-23 B.C.

NOTES ON CHAPTER III

1. This has been maintained by Archdeacon Allen and Professor Wellhausen in connexion with S. Mark's Gospel, and recently Canon Burney has published an important study on *The Aramaic Origin of the Fourth Gospel* (Oxford, 1922).

2. R. Rothe, *Zur Dogmatik* (Gotha, 1863), p. 238 f.: "We can indeed with good right speak of a language of

the Holy Ghost. For in the Bible it is manifest to our eyes how the Divine Spirit at work in revelation always takes the language of the particular people chosen to be the recipient and makes of it a characteristic religious variety by transforming existing linguistic elements and existing conceptions into a shape peculiarly appropriate to that Spirit. This process is shown most clearly by the Greek of the New Testament " (as quoted by Deissmann, *The Philology of the Greek Bible* (London, Hodder and Stoughton, 1908), p. 42 f.).

3. It is impossible to discuss here the history of the Koinē, but reference may be made to Dr. J. H. Moulton's *Grammar of New Testament Greek*, 3rd Edit. (Edinburgh, T. & T. Clark, 1908), i. *Prolegomena*, especially chapter ii., and to the same writer's Essay on " New Testament Greek in the light of modern discovery " in *Essays on some Biblical Questions of the Day* (London, Macmillan, 1909), p. 461 ff.

Much valuable material bearing on the Greek of the New Testament generally will be found in J. de Zwaan's chapter on " The Use of the Greek Language in Acts " and W. K. L. Clarke's chapter on " The Use of the Septuagint in Acts " in *The Beginnings of Christianity*, Part I., vol. ii., edited by F. J. Foakes Jackson and Kirsopp Lake (London, Macmillan, 1922).

4. Cf. J. Rendel Harris, *The Expository Times*, xxv. p. 54 f., and notes by the present writer in *ib.* xxxi. p. 421, and xxxii. p. 231 f.

Of a much more general character, but interesting from its early date, is Dr. John Lightfoot's comment on the Preface to the Lord's Prayer in Matt. vi. 9 in his *Horae Hebraicae et Talmudicae*, first published as far back as

1658: " In interpreting very many phrases and histories of the New Testament, it is not so much worth, what we think of them from notions of our own, feigned upon I know not what grounds, as in what sense these things were understood by the hearers and lookers on, according to the usual custom and vulgar dialect of the nation."

5. I owe the reference to a note by W. L. Lorimer of St. Andrews University in *The Expository Times*, xxxii. p. 330, where reference is also made to the position taken up by Salmasius in his *Funus linguae Hellenisticae* and his *De Hellenistica Commentarius*, both published in 1643.

6. The passage was communicated by the Rev. J. Pulliblank to Professor J. H. Moulton, and was published by him in the second edition of the *Prolegomena* (1906), p. 242.

7. *New Testament Documents*, p. 70 ff. Many interesting points are graphically dealt with by Dr. J. H. Moulton in his volume of popular lectures on the New Testament, entitled *From Egyptian Rubbish-Heaps* (London, Kelly, 1916). See also Maurice Jones, *The New Testament in the Twentieth Century* (London, Macmillan, 1914), chap. viii., " The Language of the New Testament," and E. Jacquier, *Études de Critique et de Philologie du Nouveau Testament* (Paris, Lecoffre, 1920), chap. iii., " La Langue du Nouveau Testament."

8. *Turin Papyri*, i. No. 1,[l. 19 ff.] (116 B.C.) τῶν τούτων ἀδελφῶν τῶν τὰς λειτουργίας ἐν ταῖς νεκρίαις παρεχομένων. *Paris Papyri*, No. 42^1 (156 B.C.) Βαρκαῖος καὶ Ἀπολλώνιος Ἀπολλωνίῳ τῷ ἀδελφῷ χαίρειν.

9. The passages cited are from *Tebtunis Papyri*, i. No. 40 (=*Selections*, No. 10), *Berliner Griechische Ur-*

kunden, i. No. 22 (=*Selections*, No. 29), and *ib.* i. No. 16 (=*Selections*, No. 33).

10. The story of the Twins has been graphically reconstructed by Sir F. G. Kenyon in *British Museum Papyri*, i. p. 2 ff.

11. *Oxyrhynchus Papyri*, iv. No. 731.

12. *Hibeh Papyri*, i. No. 78[11] (244-3 B.C.).

13. *Oxyrhynchus Papyri*, i. No. 40 (ii/iii A.D.).

14. *Paris Papyri*, No. 58[14] (ii/B.C.). *Greek Papyri*, Series ii., edited by B. P. Grenfell and A. S. Hunt, No. 67[17] (237 A.D.) (=*Selections*, No. 45).

15. *Rylands Papyri*, ii. No. 243[11] (ii/A.D.). This same papyrus supplies good examples of λόγος, "account," and of the common legal phrase τὸ ἐπιβάλλον μέρος, as in Luke xv. 12—δέξαι παρὰ Νιννάρου ἰς λόγον Εἰρήνης τὸ ἐπιβάλλον αὐτῇ μέρος, "receive from Ninnarus for Irene's account the share belonging to her" (Edd.).

16. *Berliner Griechische Urkunden*, i. No. 140[31 f.] (119 A.D.).

17. *Amherst Papyri*, ii. No. 85[20 ff.]

18. *Oxyrhynchus Papyri*, ix. No. 1200[29 f.]

19. For this legal sense of ὑπόστασις see *Oxyrhynchus Papyri*, ii. No. 237 [viii. 20] (186 A.D.) with the editors' note (p. 176): "ὑπόστασις, of which the central meaning is 'substance,' i.e. property, ... is used here for the whole body of documents bearing on the ownership of a person's property whether ἀπογραφαί, sales, mortgages, etc.) deposited in the archives, and forming the evidence of ownership."

20. *Berliner Griechische Urkunden*, i. No. 249[21].

21. *Oxyrhynchus Papyri*, vi. No. 932[51.] (late ii/A.D.). Other instances of this interesting verb of a more general character may be added. In *Hibeh Papyri*, i. No. 39 (265 (264) B.C.), with reference to the embarkation upon a government transport of a quantity of corn, instructions are given that the shipmaster is to write a receipt, and further " let him seal a sample (δεῖγμα σφραγισάσ[θ]ω)," obviously to prevent the corn from being tampered with during the transit (Edd.), and in *Oxyrhynchus Papyri*, i. No. 116 (ii/A.D.), the writer of the letter of consolation which will meet us again (see p. 107) writes to the same two friends: " I send you ... a box of very excellent grapes and a basket of excellent dates under seal (ἐσφραγι(σμένας)."

22. *Oxyrhynchus Papyri*, ii. No. 275 (=*Selections*, No. 20). For a fuller discussion of ἀτακτέω and its cognates see Milligan, *Thessalonians*, p. 152 ff.

23. *Petrie Papyri*, ii. No. 39 (*e*)[18] (iii/B.C.). *Greek Papyri*, Series ii., No. 14 (*b*)[2] (iii/B.C.). See also Deissmann, *Light from the Ancient East*, p. 372 ff., and Milligan, *Thessalonians*, p. 145 ff.

24. Theon's letter first appeared in *Oxyrhynchus Papyri*, i. No. 119, and has frequently been reproduced, *e.g.* in Deissmann's *Light from the Ancient East*, p. 187 ff., and in *Selections*, No. 42. For those who are not acquainted with it, the following translation will be of interest.

Theon to Theon his father greeting. So kind of you not to have taken me along with you to the city ! If you refuse to take me along with you to Alexandria, I won't write you a letter, or speak to you, or wish you health. And if you do go to Alexandria, I won't take your hand, or greet you again henceforth. If you refuse to take me, that's what's up! And my mother said to Archelaus, "He upsets me: off with him!" So kind of you to send me gifts, great ones, husks (δράκια)!! They deceived us there, on the 12th, when you sailed. Send for me then, I beseech you. If you don't send, I won't eat, I won't drink! There now (ταῦτα)! I pray for your health. Tubi 18.

(Addressed) Deliver to Theon from Theonas his son.

25. *Florence Papyri*, i. No. 99 (i/ii A.D.) (=*Selections*, No. 27). A striking parallel to our Lord's Trial before Pilate is found in another papyrus from the same collection, No. 61[59 ff.] (85 A.D.), where the Prefect, after stating with reference to a certain Phibion, "Thou hadst been worthy of scourging (ἄξιος μ[ὲ]ν ἦς μαστιγωθῆναι; cf. John xix. 1)," adds—"but I will give you freely to the multitude (χαρίζομαι δέ σε τοῖς ὄχλοις: cf. Mark **xv.** 15)": see Vitelli's note *ad l.*, and cf. Deissmann, *Light from the Ancient East*, p. 266 f.

26. *Einleitung in die drei ersten Evangelien* (Berlin, 1905), p. 9.

27. *An Introduction to the New Testament*, translated by Janet Penrose Ward (London, 1904), pp. 48 f., 51.

28. Deissmann, *Bible Studies*, p. 44.

NOTES ON CHAPTER IV.

1. See *e.g.* Dr. James Orr, *Neglected Factors in the Study of the Early Progress of Christianity*, p. 95 ff.

2. See Sir William M. Ramsay's two articles in *The Expositor*, VIII. iv. pp. 385 and 481 ff., and more recently his work *The Bearing of Recent Discovery on the Trustworthiness of the New Testament*, London, 1915, p. 222 ff. See also Lt.-Col. G. Mackinlay, *The Magi: How they recognised Christ's Star*, London, 1907, and W. M. Calder in *Discovery*, i. (1920), p. 100 ff.

3. For the Greek text see *British Museum Papyri*, No. 904 (= iii. p. 124 ff., Milligan, *Selections*, No. 28), also Deissmann, *Light from the Ancient East*, p. 268.

4. *Oxyrhynchus Papyri*, ii. No. 255 (= *Selections*, No. 17).

5. *Elephantine Papyri*, No. 1 (= *Selections*, No. 1).

6. For an example of a Deed of Divorce, see *Berliner Griechische Urkunden*, iii. No. 975 (45 A.D.) (= *Selections*, No. 16).

7. *British Museum Papyri*, No. 42 (B.C. 168) (= i. p. 29 ff., *Selections*, No. 4).

8. *Oxyrhynchus Papyri*, iii. No. 528 (ii/A.D.).

9. *Giessen Papyri*, i. No. 19. See *Journal of Egyptian Archaeology*, vi. p. 235 f.

10. *Oxyrhynchus Papyri*, iv. No. 744 (= *Selections*, No. 12).

11. *Oxyrhynchus Papyri*, vii. No. $1069^{21\,ff.}$ (iii/A.D.).

12. *Petrie Papyri*, ii. No. 11 (1) (iii/B.C.) (= *Selections*, No. 3).

13. P. Lond. Inv. No. 2102: see *Journal of Egyptian Archaeology*, vi. p. 239.

14. *Oxyrhynchus Papyri*, xii. No. 1481.

15. *Berliner Griechische Urkunden*, iii. No. 814 (iii/A.D.).

16. *Oxyrhynchus Papyri*, iii. No. 531 (ii/A.D.).

17. *Oxyrhynchus Papyri*, vi. No. 930 (ii/iii A.D.).

18. *Giessen Papyri*, i. No. 17. The Greek text will also be found in Milligan, *New Testament Documents*, p. 258.

19. *Oxyrhynchus Papyri*, xiv. No. 1676 (iii/A.D.).

20. As showing how effectively Deissmann's discussion may be used for practical purposes, reference may be made to the devotional studies from the Egyptian papyri published by the Rev. (now Archbishop) Harrington C. Lees under the title *Christ and His Slaves* (London, R. Scott, 1911).

21. *Fresh Light on Roman Bureaucracy*, p. 21; cf. *Journal of Theological Studies*, xxiii. (1922), p. 282 f. The Code referred to is published as the first part of Vol. v. of the *Berliner Griechische Urkunden*, and the section with which we are immediately concerned runs as follows: § 47: ἀστὴ συνελθοῦσα Αἰ[γ]υ[πτίῳ] κατ' ἄγνοιαν ὡς ἀστῷ ἀνεύθυνός ἐστιν. ἐὰν δὲ καὶ ὑπὸ ἀμφοτέρ[ων ἀπ]αρχὴ τέκνων τεθῇ, τηρεῖται τοῖς τέκνοις ἡ πολιτεία, " if a woman, being a citizen [*i.e.* of Alexandria], marries an Egyptian in the mistaken belief that he is also a citizen, she is not liable to penalty; and if both parties present birth-certificates, their children preserve the status of citizens " (Jones).

22. For the meaning of the papyrus (J. 383 of the Leiden Museum) see further de Zwaan in the *Journal of Theological Studies*, vi. (1905), p. 418 ff.

23. *Oxyrhynchus Papyri*, iii. No. 523 (ii/A.D.) (=*Selections*, No. 39).

24. For further examples of the religious use of κύριος see Moulton and Milligan, *Vocabulary of the Greek Testament*, s.v., and Deissmann, *Light from the Ancient East*, p. 353 ff. The frequent application of the term to Nero makes it no longer possible to claim Acts xxv. 26 as a proof of the late date of that book.

25. *Paris Papyri*, No. 61 (156 B.C.). See also Wilcken, *Griechische Ostraka* (Leipzig and Berlin, 1899), i. p. 568 f.

26. *Tebtunis Papyri*, ii. No. 315 (ii/A.D.).

27. *Rylands Papyri*, ii. No. 114.

28. *Oxyrhynchus Papyri*, i. No. 115 (ii/A.D.) (=*Selections*, No. 38).

29. *Berliner Griechische Urkunden*, iii. No. 846 (ii/A.D.) (=*Selections*, No. 37).

30. *Fayûm Papyri*, No. 137 (=*Selections*, No. 25).

31. *Fayûm Papyri*, No. 138 (i/ii A.D.).

32. P Par 574$^{1227\,ff.}$ (=*Selections*, No. 47).

33. The adj. δεισιδαίμων is strictly a neutral term (see Moulton and Milligan, *Vocabulary*, s.v.), and in the passage in Acts seems to carry with it the double connotation indicated in the text.

NOTES ON CHAPTER V.

1. The references are collected by Harnack, *The Mission and Expansion of Christianity*, 2nd Edit. (London, 1908), ii. p. 158 ff. See also P. D. Scott-Moncrieff, *Paganism and Christianity in Egypt*, Cambridge, 1913.

2. The student will find a full and clear survey of the whole field in *The New Archaeological Discoveries and their*

Bearing upon the New Testament and upon the Life and Times of the Primitive Church, by Camden M. Cobern, D.D., Litt.D. (New York and London, Funk and Wagnalls, 1917).

3. They have been described, so far as they were then published, by F. G. Kenyon, *Handbook to the Textual Criticism of the New Testament*, 2nd Edit., London, 1912, p. 41 ff. For a later list see Milligan, *New Testament Documents*, p. 248 ff.

4. *Oxyrhynchus Papyri*, i. No. 2.

5. The full text, which " does not agree at all consistently with any one of the chief authorities," will be found in *Oxyrhynchus Papyri*, x. No. 1228.

6. *Oxyrhynchus Papyri*, xv. No. 1781.

7. *Oxyrhynchus Papyri*, ii. No. 208 : cf. Gregory, *Textkritik des Neuen Testamentes*, iii. (Leipzig, 1909), p. 1085.

8. *Theologische Literaturzeitung*, 1901, p. 70 f.

9. *Amherst Papyri*, i. No. 3 (*b*).

10. *Oxyrhynchus Papyri*, iv. No. 657. One or two interesting features of the manuscript may be noted from an article contributed by J. H. Moulton to *The Methodist Recorder*, July 21, 1904 : " I am particularly glad to find the MS. back up the R.V. in iv. 2 ('because they were not united by faith ') and xii. 3 ('sinners against themselves '), In one place (xi. 4) Westcott and Hort ventured to prefer a small change [αὐτῷ for αὐτοῦ] which was against all the MSS., on the authority of Clement alone : now our MS. comes in to confirm their judgment. In xi. 35 the best MSS. have united in a small slip (" they

received women "), and we have now another to add to the company : it is a remarkable testimony to the accuracy of our oldest copies that they should so faithfully preserve manifest blunders (in the autograph ?) like this."

11. *Brief an die Hebräer, Text mit Angabe der Rhythmen*, Göttingen, 1903.

12. *Oxyrhynchus Papyri*, ii. No. 209 : cf. Deissmann, *Light from the Ancient East*, p. 232 n[1].

13. *Papiri della Società Italiana*, i. No. 3.

14. *Führer durch die Ausstellung der Papyrus Erzherzog Rainer* (Vienna, 1894), p. 129, No. 539 : cf. Wessely, *Wiener Studien*, iv. p. 198 ff., vii. p. 69 f., also *Expositor*, III. i. pp. 342, 600.

15. *Oxyrhynchus Papyri*, ii. p. 3. It may also be noted that we have here evidence from a much earlier date than was sometimes imagined of the use of such contractions as $\overline{\Theta C}$, $\overline{IHC}$, $\overline{XC}$, and so on : see *ib*. iii. No. 405.

16. See p. 53 f. and cf. Kenyon, *Palaeography of Greek Papyri*, p. 24. Schubart, *Das Buch bei den Griechen und Römern* (Berlin, 1907), p. 101 f., infers, from a Priene inscription, the existence of papyrus codices in Asia Minor about the beginning of the first century B.C.

17. *Zeitschrift für Katholische Theologie*, 1885, p. 498 ff., and, later, *Mittheilungen aus der Sammlung der Papyrus Erzherzog Rainer*, i. p. 53 ff., ii. p. 41 f.

18. *Texte und Untersuchungen*, v. 4 (1889), p. 483 ff., " Das Evangelien fragment von Fajjum."

19. Letter to *The Times*, of July 25th, 1885.

20. *Oxyrhynchus Papyri*, iv. No. 655.

21. *Oxyrhynchus Papyri*, x. No. 1224.

22. ΛΟΓΙΑ ΙΗΣΟΥ: 'Sayings of Our Lord,' from an Early Greek Papyrus. By B. P. Grenfell and A. S. Hunt (Frowde, 1897). (*Out of print.*) See also *Oxyrhynchus Papyri*, i. No. 1.

23. *New Sayings of Jesus and Fragment of a Lost Gospel*, with the text of the 'Logia' discovered in 1897. By B. P. Grenfell and A. S. Hunt (Frowde, 1904). See also *Oxyrhynchus Papyri*, iv. No. 654.

24. These can now be conveniently studied in *The Sayings of Jesus* from Oxyrhynchus, edited with Introduction, Critical Apparatus and Commentary by Hugh G. Evelyn White, M.A. (Cambridge University Press, 1920). Cf. also an article by V. Bartlet in *The Expositor*, VIII. xxiii. p. 136 ff.

25. *Uber die jungst entdeckten Sprüche Jesu*, by A. Harnack (Freiburg i. Baden, 1897): English Translation in *The Expositor*, V. vi. pp. 321 ff., 401 ff.

26. *Die jungst gefundenen " Aussprüche Jesu,"* by T. Zahn in the *Theologisches Literaturblatt*, xviii. (1897), pp. 417 ff., 425 ff.

27. *The Oxyrhynchus Logia and the Apocryphal Gospels*, by the Rev. C. Taylor (Oxford, 1899), and *The Oxyrhynchus Sayings of Jesus*, by the same (1905).

28. Cf. M. R. James in the *Contemporary Review*, lxxii. (1897), p. 156.

29. Upon the influence which these extra-evangelic documents may have had on the transmission of the text of the Canonical Gospels, see J. Rendel Harris in the *Contemporary Review*, lxxii. (1897), p. 341 ff.

30. See *e.g. The Newly-found Words of Jesus*, by W. Garrett Horder (London, 1904); *Jesus Saith*—Studies in some "New Sayings" of Christ, by J. Warschauer (London, 1905); and *Unwritten Sayings of our Lord*, by David Smith (London [1913]).

31. For these documents see *Oxyrhynchus Papyri*, iii. No. 405; *ib.* ii. No. 210; *ib.* i. No. 5 (cf. Harnack, *Die Chronologie der Altchristlichen Litteratur bis Eusebius*, ii. p. 181); *ib.* i. No. 4 (cf. Harnack, *Chronologie*, ii. p. 181); *ib.* viii. No. 1081.

32. *Mittheilungen aus der Sammlung der Papyrus Erzherzog Rainer*, ii. p. 83 ff. Cf. Stokes in *The Expositor*, III. vii. p. 456.

33. *Amherst Papyri*, i. No. 2, and for a fuller restoration of the text see C. Wessely, *Les plus anciens Monuments du Christianisme écrits sur Papyrus* (in *Patrologia Orientalis*, iv. 2), p. 205 ff.

34. *Sitzungsberichte der Akademie zu Berlin*, 1900, p. 986 f.

35. *Oxyrhynchus Papyri*, xv. No. 1786.

36. *Berliner Klassiker Texte*, vi. (1910), p. 110 ff.

37. *Oxyrhynchus Papyri*, iii. No. 407.

38. *Oxyrhynchus Papyri*, vii. No. 1058, ὁ θ(εὸ)ς τῶν παρακειμένων σταυρῶν, βοήθησον τὸν δοῦλόν σου ᾽Απφουᾶν. ἀμήν.

39. *Oxyrhynchus Papyri*, vii. No. 1059 (v/A.D.).

40. The prayers are edited by C. Schmidt in *Neutestamentliche Studien Georg Heinrici zu seinem 70 Geburtstag dargebracht* (Leipzig, 1914), p. 66 ff.

41. *Rylands Papyri*, i. No. 6.

42. *Oxyrhynchus Papyri*, xv. No. 1784.

43. *Greek Papyri chiefly Ptolemaic*, No. 53.

44. *Oxyrhynchus Papyri*, xiii. No. 1603.

45. *Greek Papyri*, Series ii., No. 111.

46. *Oxyrhynchus Papyri*, xi. No. 1357.

47. See Deissmann, *Light from the Ancient East*, p. 332, where reference is also made to the pagan phrase found in *Oxyrhynchus Papyri*, i. Nos. 48, 49 (as amended)—ὑπὸ Δία Γῆν Ἥλιον ἐπὶ λύτροις, " under Zeus, Earth, Sun, for a ransom."

48. *Rylands Papyri*, i. No. 12. For another specimen see *Berliner Griechische Urkunden*, i. No. 287, reproduced in *Selections*, No. 48, with references to the relevant literature.

49. Cf. Scott-Moncrieff, *Paganism and Christianity in Egypt*, p. 88.

50. *Amherst Papyri*, i. No. 3 (*a*); see also Wessely, *Monuments*, p. 135 ff.

51. *Light from the Ancient East*, p. 200.

52. The letter was originally published in *Greek Papyri*, Series ii. No. 73. Deissmann's study was published under the title *Ein Original-Dokument aus der Diocletianischen Christenverfolgung*, Tübingen, 1902 (English Translation, London, A. & C. Black, 1902 and 1907). In support of their interpretation of πολιτική, Grenfell and Hunt can now point to *Oxyrhynchus Papyri*, vi. No. 903[37], where the word is clearly = πόρνη.

53. *Oxyrhynchus Papyri*, vi. No. 939 (=*Selections*, No. 53).

54. *British Museum Papyri*, No. 417 (=ii. p. 299 f., *Selections*, No. 51).

55. *Oxyrhynchus Papyri*, vi. No. 925 (v/vi A.D.).

56. For another example see *Berliner Griechische Urkunden*, iii. No. 954 (=*Selections*, No. 55).

57. *Oxyrhynchus Papyri*, viii. No. 1152, Ωρωρ φωρ ἐλωεί, ἀδωναεί, Ἰαὼ σαβαώθ, Μιχαήλ, Ἰεσοῦ Χριστέ, βοήθι ἡμῖν καὶ τούτῳ οἴκῳ. ἀμήν.

For an interesting modern parallel we may compare the document which was found sewn into Pascal's doublet after his death. It is dated " Monday, the 23rd of November, 1654, between half past ten at night and half-past twelve," and begins—

Fire.

God of Abraham, God of Isaac, God of Jacob—
Not of philosophers or the wise—
Certainty, Certainty, Feeling, Joy, Peace.

Here and There among the Papyri

1. *Authors and Subjects*

Abbott-Smith, G., x
Addresses of N.T. writings, 29 ff.
Aegyptus, 154
Agrapha, 127
Allen, W. C., 158
Amulets, 119, 150 ff.
Arnold, M., 84
Authenticating signature, 40 f.
Autographs, N.T., 27 ff.

Bacchylides, 13
Barber, E. A., 154
Bartlet, V., 169
Bell, H. I., 17, 91 f.
Bereavement, 106 ff.
Bickell, 123 ff., 134
Blass, 119
Buell, 157
Burney, C. F., 158

Calder, W. M., 164
Census papers, 85 ff.
Charta Borgiana, 10, 153
Chinese writers, 44 f.

Christian letters, 144 ff.
Christianity in Egypt, 113 f.
Church organization, 139 ff.
Clarke, W. K. L., 159
Cobern, C. M., 167
Codex, Papyrus, 53 f., 122 f.
Common people, 82 ff.
Consolation, letter of, 106 ff.
Constitution of Athens, 13
Contract of apprenticeship, 74 f.
Contractions in MSS., 168
Copying, 48 f.
Corinthians, 2nd Ep. to, 52
Cratippus, 19
Creeds, 138 f.
Cyprian, 142

Deissmann, xi, 57, 69, 70, 73, 99, 101, 117, 119, 145, 146 f., 156, 158, 162, 163, 166, 171
Delivery of N.T. writings, 30
Dictation, 38 ff.
Didache, 135

Divorce, 90, 164
Donaldson, Sir James, 60 f.

Education, 96 f.
Ephorus, 19
Epistolary form, 33 ff., 37
Euripides, 20
Evangelistarium, 120
Evil eye, 97

Family life, 89 ff.
Farrar, 62
Forshall, J., 62
Fox, George, 156

Galatians, Ep. to, 29, 30 f., 41 ff.
Goodspeed, E. J., 18
Graeco-Roman World, 84 f.
Grammar, N.T., x f., 79
Greek: 'common,' 55 ff.; real character of, 57 ff.
Gregory, C. R., 167
Grenfell, B. P., x, 13, 117, 122, 129, 154, 160, 171

Harnack, 125, 130, 132, 166
Harris, J. Rendel, 157, 159, 169
Headlam, 72
Hebraisms, 56 f.
Hebrews, Ep. to, 31
Helbing, ix
Herculaneum Papyri, 7, 153
Herondas, 13
Homeric texts, 7, 19

Horder, W. G., 170
Hort, 125
Howard, W. F., x
Hunt, A. S., x, 13, 17, 21, 117, 122, 129, 150, 161, 171
Husbands and wives, 89 ff.
Hymns, 135 f.
Hyperides, 11

Jacquier, E., 160
James, M. R., 169
Johnson, J. de M., 17
Jones, Maurice, 160
Jones, Stuart, 99 f., 165
Journal of Egyptian Archaeology, x
Jülicher, 80 f.

Kenyon, Sir F. G., 17, 20, 28, 153, 154, 161, 167, 168
Koinē, 24 f., 58

Lees, Archbishop, 165
Legal documents, 70 ff.
Letters of commendation, 33 ff.
Lexicography, N.T., x
Libelli, 142 ff.
Lietzmann, ix
Lightfoot, J., 159 f.
Lightfoot, Bishop J. B., 31, 61 f., 78
Liturgical works, 133 f.
Liturgy, 66 f.
Lorimer, W. L., 169

Luther, 153
Lysias, 19

Mackinlay, G., 164
Magical papyri, 110 ff., 151
Mahaffy, Sir J. P., 11, 17
Manumission, 99, 141
Mark, Gospel of, ending of, 50 f.
Martin, V., 17, 155
Masson, Prof., 59 f.
M'Lean, N., 155
Menander, 19
Mitteis, ix
Moule, Bishop, 157
Moulton, J. H., x, xi, 58, 79, 159, 160, 166, 167

New Testament: language of, 55 ff.; as literature, 79 ff.; surroundings of, 82 ff.
Non-canonical texts, 123 ff.

Orr, J., 163
Oxyrhynchus Papyri, x

Papias, 125
Papyri: classification of, 19 ff.; collections of, 15 ff.; discoveries of, 7 ff.
Papyrus: as a writing material, 2 ff.; Christian documents on, 113 ff.; New Testament texts on, 15, 115 ff.

Parents and children, 92 ff.
Parousia, 75 f.
Pascal, 172
Pauline Epistles: form of, 32 ff.; differences of language and style of, 44; literary character of, 80 f.
Pedagogue, 97
Persae, 7
Peter, Gospel of, 128
Petitions, 105 f.
Petrie, Flinders, 11
Philemon, Ep. to, 149
Philodemus, 153
Pindar, 20
Pirke Aboth, 131
Pliny, 153
Postal Service, State, 155 f.
Powell, J. U., 154
Prayers, 136 ff.
Presbyter, 65 f.
Prodigal son, 108 f.
Pulliblank, J., 160

Questions in temples, 109 f.; in churches, 149 f.
Quirinius, 86 f.
Quotation, 49

Ramsay, Sir W. M., 31, 32, 67, 86, 156, 164
Reading of N.T. rolls, 47 f.
Receipts, 68 f.
Recto, 3
Robertson, A. T., xi, 79
Robinson, J. A., 157

Romans, Ep. to, ending of, 51 f.
Rothe, 158 f.

Salmasius, 160
Sanday, 48 f., 72
Sappho, 20
'Sayings' of Jesus, 14, 128 ff.
Schmidt, C., 170
Schow, N., 153
Schubart, W., xii, 155, 168
Scott-Moncrieff, P. D., 166, 171
Sealing, 72 f.
Septuagint, 22, 56
Shorthand, 45 ff.
Signature, authenticating, 40 ff.
Sin, 108 f.
Slaves, 97 ff.
Smith, D., 170
Smyly, J. G., 17
Social life, 101 ff.
Souter, A., x
Spirit: earnest of, 68; first fruits of, 99 f.
Stigmata, 100 f.

Structure, questions of, 50 ff.
Synoptic problem, 48

Taxation, 103 ff.
Taylor, C., 130
Tertius, 40
Texts, N.T., 115 ff.
Thackeray, St. John, xi
Theological works, 132 f.
Theopompus, 19
Title-deeds, 72
Tyrrell, R. Y., 154

Verso, 3
Vocabulary, N.T., 63 ff.

Warschauer, 170
Wellhausen, 80, 158
Wessely, 168, 170, 171
White, H. G. E., 169
Wilcken, ix, 153, 154, 166
Witkowski, ix, 155
Wordsworth, 13
Writing materials, 5

Zahn, 130
Zwaan, J. de, 159, 165

2. New Testament References

St. Matthew	Page
i. 1	116
ii. 11, 22	110
v. 24	108
v. 31	90
vi. 16	69, 91
vii. 3 ff.	14
vii. 17 ff.	132
ix. 9	103
xii. 48	65
xxiii. 8	65
xxvi. 32	124

St. Mark	Page
xiv. 26 ff.	123
xvi. 9 ff.	50

St. Luke	Page
i. 1 f.	125
ii. 1 ff.	86 ff.
ii. 49	102 f.
iii. 14	95, 104
vi. 28	78
vi. 43 f.	132
vii. 36 ff.	120
x. 38 ff.	120
xi. 37	102
xv. 13	78
xv. 18, 21	108 f.
xviii. 3	106
xix. 8	104

St. John	Page
i. 23 ff.	117
iii. 14 ff.	120
iii. 31 f.	120
xv. 25 ff.	116
xvi. 21 ff.	116
xix. 5	78
xx. 11 ff.	117
xx. 19 ff.	117
xxi. 1 ff.	117

Acts	Page
ii. 29, 37	65
v. 37	86
xvii. 6	77
xvii. 22	111
xxi. 36	78
xxii. 22	78
xxiii. 26	34
xxv. 26	166
xxviii. 9	67

Romans	Page
i. 1 ff.	119
v. 13	70
viii. 18 ff.	81

viii. 23	99 f.
xv. 28	72
xvi. 1 ff.	51 f.
xvi. 22	40

1 Corinthians

i. 7 f.	71
i. 16 f.	43
i. 26 f.	83
viii. 5 f.	102
x. 21	102
xiii. 1 ff.	81
xv. 31	98
xvi. 21 ff.	41

2 Corinthians

i-ix.	52
i. 22	68, 72
iii. 1	33
iv. 7	112
v. 5	68
vii. 8	52
ix. 12	68
x.-xiii.	52
xi. 8	93

Galatians

i. 24	97
iii. 1	78, 97
v. 12	77
vi. 11	42 f.
vi. 17	100 f.

Ephesians

i. 3 ff.	43
i. 13	72
i. 14	68
i. 15 ff.	43

Philippians

i. 12	108
ii. 9	102
ii. 17, 30	68
iv. 18	69

Colossians

ii. 14	5
iv. 18	41

1 Thessalonians

i. 1	34
iv. 1	93, 102
iv. 13 f.	108
v. 27	43
v. 28	34

2 Thessalonians

iii. 11	74
iii. 17 f.	40
iii. 18	34

Philemon

1 ff.	149
15	69
18	70

Hebrews

i. 1	118
iv. 2	167
xi. 1	72

New Testament References

	PAGE		PAGE
xi. 35	167	3 JOHN	
xii. 3	167	15	97
2 JOHN		REVELATION	
1	94	iii. 5	5
12	5	v. 1	3

3. Greek Words

ἀβάσκαντος, 97
ἀγράμματος, 157
ἀδελφός, 64, 160
ἀθυμέω, 128
αἴρω, 77 f.
αἰσχύνω, 127
ἀλείφω, 91
ἀλεκτρύων, 124
ἁμαρτάνω, 108
ἀναγινώσκω, 43, 46
ἀναστατόω, 77
ἀπαρχή, 99 f., 165
ἀπέχω, 68 ff.
ἀποκάλυψις, 76
ἀπόρροια, 133
ἀρραβών, 68
ἀτακτέω, 74, 162
ἀτάκτως, 74
ἀφανίζω, 91

βασκαίνω, 97
βαστάζω, 101
βέβαιος, 70 ff.

βεβαιόω, 71
βεβαίωσις, 71
βίβλιον, 140
βραδέως, 39
βρόχιον, 5

γινώσκω, 108
γράμμα, 42

δαίμων, 90
δεισιδαίμων, 111, 166
διαλλάσσω, 108
δωτήρ, 136

ἐκβάλλω, 93
ἐκδύω, 127
ἐλλογάω, 70
ἐλλογέω, 70
ἐμφανής, 126
ἔννοια, 133
ἐξαλείφω, 5
ἐπηρεάζω, 78
ἐπιβάλλω, 161

ἐπιβαρέω, 95
ἐπιφάνεια, 76
ἐρωτάω, 93, 102

ἡγεμονεύω, 87

θεραπεύω, 67

καθηγητής, 96
κάλαμος, 5
κάρφος, 14
κοκκύζω, 124
κόπος, 101
κύριος, 94, 102, 166

λειτουργέω, 66 ff.
λειτουργία, 160
λόγος, 161
λύτρον, 171

μαστιγόω, 163
μέρος, 161

νεκρία, 160

ὄνομα, 97
ὄπισθεν, 4
ὀχλέω, 94
ὄχλος, 163
ὀψώνιον, 67, 93

παιδαγωγός, 97
παιδίσκη, 93

πάπας, 149
παρακαλέω, 93
παράκειμαι, 170
παρέχω, 101
παρουσία, 75
πεζοῦ, 46
πήλικος, 42
πολιτεία, 165
πολιτική, 146, 171
πρεσβύτερος, 65, 139
προγράφω, 78 f.
προπάτωρ, 133

σαββατικός, 138
σημειογράφος, 46
σταυρός, 170
στίγμα, 101
στρατεύομαι, 95
συκοφαντέω, 103
συστατικός, 33
σφραγίζω, 72½f.

ταῦτα, 163
τελωνία, 103

ὑπόστασις, 72, 161

φιλοπονέω, 93

χαρίζομαι, 163
χάρτιον, 4, 140, 153
χειρόγραφον, 5
χρηματίζω, 110

www.ingramcontent.com/pod-product-compliance
Lightning Source LLC
Chambersburg PA
CBHW051926160426
43198CB00012B/2058